To Jamie

don't look
down for
too long

KAY

presents
**The Sir Barry Jackson
Community Tour 2000**

My Dad's Corner Shop
by Ray Grewal

OPEN

First performance
in the community at
**Handsworth Wood Girls School,
West Midlands**
on **6 March 2000**

First performance in
The Door
on **29 March 2000**

SUPPORTED BY
THE NATIONAL LOTTERY
THROUGH
THE ARTS COUNCIL
OF ENGLAND

THE
SIR BARRY JACKSON
TRUST

Birmingham City Council

WEST
MIDLANDS
ARTS

Providing Theatre for Birmingham

the door

The Door's programme seeks
to find a young and culturally
diverse audience for the
theatre, through the
production of new work in
an intimate, flexible space -
work that reflects, defines
and enhances their experience
of the world while introducing
them to the possibilities of
the medium.

Birmingham Repertory Theatre
Centenary Square, Broad Street,
Birmingham B1 2EP
Administration: 0121 245 2000
Fax: 0121 245 2100
Box Office: 0121 236 4455
www.birmingham-rep.co.uk

Artistic Director   Bill Alexander
Executive Producer   John Stalker
Associate Artistic Director Anthony Clark

Tickets: £9.00
Concs: £6.00
Standby: £5.00
Mad To Miss Mondays:
All tickets £2.99 for under 26s

Birmingham Repertory Theatre
and Hampstead Theatre

Terracotta

A Bittersweet Comedy by Jess Walters

Wed 8 Mar - Sat 25 Mar

*'Just think, I could make... passion.
I could make you passion in a paint'*

It's summer in South London and Nicola, a girl in her late teens, has escaped to her rooftop to pursue the perfect tan - alone. But Roger's got other plans and when Ian arrives from Birmingham to decorate her flat, the outlook for Nicola's day takes an unexpected turn.

Terracotta vividly captures the razor sharp emotions and changing moods of young people on the brink of adulthood. This is a bittersweet play about the pain of family relationships and the strange colours of love.

Jess Walters' recently produced plays include *Cockroach, Who?* at the Royal Court Theatre in the West End and *Ultra Violet* for the Royal Court Young People's Theatre at the Duke of York's Theatre, London.

Director: Marianne Elliot
Design: Emily Cooper

After Dark: Wed 22 March

Birmingham Repertory Theatre

My Dad's Corner Shop

A Comedy by Ray Grewal

Wed 29 Mar - Sat 8 Apr

*'We're gonna do something that's
gonna let the world know we're here!'*

Rajesh is into weight training, hard work and book-keeping. His brother Kumar is into high fashion, mucking about and 'finding his focus'. Left in charge of the family's shop whilst their parents go to India, things are going predictably badly. That is, until Rajesh empties the wheelie-bin and is apparently abducted by aliens.

My Dad's Corner Shop is an hilarious look at learning to fulfil your dreams - and discovering dreams you didn't know you had.

Ray Grewal was born and brought up in Wolverhampton. He has worked on series such as *The Bill* and *Peak Practice* and this is his first stage play.

My Dad's Corner Shop is on tour to community venues around the region from 6-24 March and 10-14 April. The Rep Community Tour is supported by the Sir Barry Jackson Trust.

Director: Rufus Norris
Design: Jane Singleton

After Dark: Wed 5 April

the door

Birmingham Repertory Theatre

Quarantine

A novel by Jim Crace
Adapted by Ben Payne

Thur 27 Apr - Sat 20 May

'So, here, be well again'

Two thousand years ago, four travellers walk into the Judaean wilderness for forty days and nights to fast and pray for miracles. Instead they encounter the imposing figure of the elegant, captivating, terrifying merchant, Musa.

But there is another traveller in the desert - a young man from Galilee who it seems, can perform miracles. Will he turn out to be their salvation?

This is the first stage adaptation of Jim Crace's compelling and imaginative novel which won the 1997 Whitbread Novel Award.

Jim Crace lives in Birmingham and is the author of *Continent*, *The Gift of Stones*, *Arcadia* and *Signals of Distress*. His most recent novel *Being Dead* was published last autumn to wide critical acclaim.

Director: Bill Alexander

After Dark: Wed 10 May

Birmingham Repertory Theatre

The Gift

A new drama by Roy Williams

Thur 25 May - Sat 17 Jun

'Yu gwan on about love, you can't even si love when it right under yer nose'

Since their childhood, when Heather left Jamaica to start a new life in England, her half-sister Bernice always claimed to have 'the gift' of raising spirits from the dead. Thirty years later when Heather returns to the island, after the murder of her much-loved son, she offers the deeds of the family house, if Bernice can bring him back...

Roy Williams' previous plays include *No Boys' Cricket Club*, *Lift Off* and *Starstruck*, for which he won the Alfred Fagon writing award in 1998.

After Dark: Wed 7 June

ᵀᴴᴱREP

My Dad's Corner Shop
By Ray Grewal

Cast

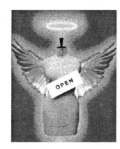

Rajesh
Anil Desai

Kumar
Raj Ghatak

Grandmother
Adlyn Ross

Angel
Nathalie Armin

Director
Rufus Norris

Designer
Jane Singleton

Lighting
Symon Harner

Sound
Dean Whiskens

Stage Manager
Richard Greville Watson

Deputy Stage Manager
Martin Pickard

Tour Technician
Steve Porter

Production Credits

Subsidised rehearsal facilities
provided by the Jerwood Space

St.George's Newtown

All costumes, properties
and settings produced by the
Birmingham Repertory
Theatre Company.

Biographies

Rajesh
Anil Desai

Theatre: The Detective in *What Shall We Do With the Body?* (The Man in the Moon); Batman/Spiderman in *Superheroes* (Quickchange Productions); Shaam/Maan in *One Night* (Moti Roti/Theatre Royal Stratford East); VP in *Comers* (Etcetera Theatre); Janga in *The Simpleton of the Unexpected Isles* (The Orange Tree); Harry in *The Cruise* (Watermans Arts Centre); Mirad in *Mirad a Boy From Bosnia* (National Theatre Studio); Maurice in *Deathwatch* (Southwark Playhouse); Pete in *The Promised Land* (Young Vic); Clark in *Hanky Panky* (Tricycle Theatre); Joey in *Road* (Cockpit Theatre).

TV: Various roles in the sketch shows *Mango Time* (Quickchange Productions) and *Goodness Gracious Me* (BBC); Tommy in *The Drive* (Anglia TV); Sumit in *The Bill* (Thames).

Film: The lead roles of Julini in *Better Late than Never* (Chulo Films), Tim in *Pens, Guns and Global Funds* (Skeleton Crew Films) and Mohit in *Phoenix* (BBC/Crucial Films).

Commercials: *totaljobs.com; Royal Navy.*

Kumar
Raj Ghatak

Training: Central School of Speech & Drama and Queen Mary Westfield College.

Theatre: Various roles in the comedy sketch show *Airport 2000* (Greenwich Theatre); First British Asian male to appear in a West End musical playing Nibbles/ Chino in *West Side Story* (Prince of Wales, West End); Gurmal in *Bollywood or Bust* (Tabularasa Arts/Watermans Arts Centre); *Arrange that Marriage* and *Don't Look at my Sister-Innit!* (National Tour for One Nation Under a Groove-Innit!!); Saleem in *East is East* (Oldham Coliseum); Sole UK representative at World Drama Festival in Jerusalem; Ala-din in *Ala-din and the Wonderful Lamp* (Paul Robeson Theatre); Nagaji in *Nagwanti* (UK tour with Tara Arts); Agisthus in *Agamemnon*; Bernie in *Sexual Perversity in Chicago*; Hilary in *The Old Country*.

TV: *Out of Sight* (Carlton); *Crimewatch* (BBC); *Eastenders* (BBC); *Grange Hill* (BBC); *Casualty* (BBC); *In No Time* (BBC2); *Hotel Babylon* (Channel 4).

Film: *Birthday Girl* (Portobello Pictures); *Saris and Trainers* (Stretch Limo Productions); *The Escort* (Pathè Productions).

Pop videos include: *Marcella Detroit, Take That* and the *Bee Gees.*

Raj also has modelling credits and has recorded numerous voice-overs in England, Europe and India.

Grandmother
Adlyn Ross

Place of Birth: Calcutta

Training: Guildhall School of Music and Drama

Theatre: *Dream for a Hero* (Lyric, Hammersmith); Baa in *Bravely Fought the Queen* (British Premiere & National Tour); Devi in *Emeralds and Diamonds*; Maria in *Twelfth Night* (National and British Council Overseas Tours).

TV: Minder (ITV/Euston Films); Dr Pamani in *Kinsey* (BBC); Mrs Siddiqui in *My Sister Wife* (BBC Screen 2); Govina in *Casualty* (BBC); Mrs Chandra in *Heartburn Hotel* (series for BBC).

Film: Ranjit's mother in *Bhaji on the Beach* (Umbi Films); Rehana in *Flight* (Black Screen/BBC Screen 2); Mother in *Guru in Seven*.

Radio: *Untouchable*; Chachee in House of the Sun; Asimun in Beyond Purdah; Mrs Kanju and Old Prostitute in *Good Woman of Ajmeer*; Bauchis in *Seven Dams*.

Angel
Nathalie Armin

Training: Central School of Speech and Drama

Theatre: Laura Lee in *Natural World* (Oval Theatre and tour); *St Pancreas Chambers Project* (London International Festival of Theatre); Mina Harker in *Dracula* (Regent's Park); Anya in *Small Objects of Desire* (Soho Theatre Company); The Messenger in *Oedipus Table* (Finborough Theatre).

TV: *Randall & Hopkirk Deceased* (Working Title/Ghost Productions); *Casualty* (BBC); *Maisie Raine* (BBC); *Deep Secrets* (Granada); T*he Crime* (BBC); *Hands* (Thames).

Radio: For BBC Radio 4, *The Glad House*; *Psyche*; *Keep on Running*.

Biographies

Ray Grewal
Author

Education: Media Production 1st Class Honours Degree (Commendation in Scriptwriting), University of Northumbria at Newcastle (1992-1995).

Training: Sept 1996-Mar 1997 Birmingham Repertory Theatre Attachment Scheme for Writers; Oct 1996-Jan1997 Carlton UK Screenwriting Course (Drama); 1998 Performing Arts Lab.

Film & TV: *A2Z* (Spitfire Films, series in development with Channel 4); *Redemption* (short listed for production by Tyne Tees Television); *Marvin, I Don't Wanna Be Dead* (short listed for production by CESC/Central Television); *Piano Player* (written as part of the Carlton Screenwriter's Course); *Alice's Restaurant* (Golden Square Pictures); *Poona Company* (in development with Endboard Productions); *Peak Practice* (Storylined one episode for Carlton).

Rufus Norris
Director

Rufus works freelance alongside running his own company, Wink. Productions include *About the Boy*; *Clubbed Out*; *Back2Back*; *Where the Devils Dwell* (Royal Court); *Strike Gently*; *The Art of Random Whistling*; *The People Downstairs* (Wink/Young Vic); *Small Craft Warnings* (Pleasance); *The Measles* (Gate), and several national tours for Wink including *The Lizzie Play* and *Rosa Carnivora*. Opera includes *Pierrot* and *Shawna* and *Ron's Half Moon* (ENO Baylis Programme).

⁺ʰᵉREP

Jane Singleton
Designer

Training: Motley Theatre Design Course

Theatre: *Small Craft Warnings* (The Pleasance Theatre, London); *The Rib Cage* (Manchester Royal Exchange Studio); *By Many Wounds* (The Chelsea Arts Centre); *Outside on the Street* (The Gate Theatre); *Marry Me a Little* (Bridewell Theatre); *Creamy* (The Red Room); *Trouble Sleeping* (Warehouse Theatre); *Wolves and Sheep* (Drama Centre); *Lady Betty* (ICA Theatre).

Opera: *Dido and Aeneas* and *The Turn of the Screw* (Broomhill Opera); *The Cenci* (Almeida Opera Festival).

TV: *Nights Out at the Empire* (Channel 4).

Film: *Let the Good Times Roll* (Design Assistant).

Symon Harner
Lighting Designer

For Birmingham Repertory Theatre: The World Premieres of *The Tenant of Wildfell Hall and East Lynne; A Shaft of Sunlight* (For Tamasha Theatre Company); *Playing by the Rules* (also at the Drill Hall, London); *Turn of the Screw*; National tours of *Metamorphosis* and Kafka's *Dick* (the latter being in collaboration with Lennie Tucker); *The Trial* (for The Mouse People) and *The Canal Ghost*. For The Door: *Perpetua; Trips; The Transmissions Festival; Silence* at Plymouth Theatre Royal and *My Best Friend* at The Rep (both re-lights of designs by Tim Mitchell).

For the Birmingham Rep Youth Workshop: *Pinocchio; The Threepenny Opera; Tony Harrison's 'V'*; and *The Magic Toyshop* (also at the Edinburgh Festival in collaboration with Philip Swoffer).

For Plymouth Theatre Royal: *Tales From the Vienna Woods* and *The Hired Man*.

New Writing at The Rep

In recent years the theatre has produced a range of popular, award winning and critically acclaimed new plays. These include *Divine Right* (1996), Peter Whelan's examination of the future of the British monarchy, Kate Dean's *Rough* (1994), Bryony Lavery's *Nothing Compares to You* (1995), Debbie Isitt's *Squealing Like a Pig* 1996), Ayub Khan-Din's *East is East* (co-production with Tamasha Theatre Company and the Royal Court Theatre London), Ken Blakeson's *True Brit* (1997), Nick Stafford's *The Whisper of Angels' Wings* (1997), *Frozen* by Bryony (1998) Lavery won the TMA Barclays Theatre Award for Best New Play and the Eileen Anderson/Central Drama Award and the Theatre's annual co-production with Tamasha Theatre Company *Balti Kings* by Sudha Bhuchar and Shaheem Khan.

In autumn 1998 thanks to funding from the Arts Council Stabilisation Scheme we were able to start programming our former studio space, now renamed The Door with a year round programme of new work. Plays produced include: *Confidence* by Judy Upton, *Twins* by Maureen Lawrence and Kate Dean's *Down Red Lane*, *Perpetua* by Fraser Grace (winner of the 1996 Verity Bargate award) and *All That Trouble That We Had* by Paul Lucas.

Our autumn season 1999 opened with *Silence* by Moira Buffini followed by *A Time of Fire*, the UK debut for Ugandan author Charles Mulekwa

The Theatre aims to provide a challenging, entertaining and diverse season of ten new plays, including a tour to arts and community venues in the West Midlands (this year's production is *My Dad's Corner Shop* by Ray Grewal).

In July 2000 we will be presenting Transmissions 2, a festival of work by young playwrights from the West Midlands aged 12-25.

For further information on any of the above please contact Caroline Jester, Literary Officer on 0121 245 2000

Rachel Sanders as Yemma
Silence by Moira Buffini
Photo: Stuart Hollis

From Page to Stage

An opportunity for students to participate in the process of putting on a season of new plays. Access to the country's most contemporary theatre writers , and a chance to work with directors, actors and qualified teachers in exploring a season of cutting edge theatre.

What's On Offer?

Programme One
My Best Friend by Tasmin Oglesby; *Terracotta* by Jess Walters; *My Dad's Corner Shop* by Ray Grewal. Price per student is £16.00 for 3 plays.

Programme Two
Quarantine adapted by Ben Payne from the novel by Jim Crace and *The Gift* by Roy Williams at £12.00 per student for both plays.

Workshops
On making block bookings, two workshops will be offered. The first involves an exploration of the content of the text; themes and structure etc. to be led by the Rep's Education Department and held at your college. The second will be run by the writers and directors, and will explore ideas behind the writing and the process of producing the piece from page to stage. These second workshops will take place at the theatre

After Darks
You can choose to come to the shows which are followed by an After Dark (although you are free to choose when you want to come). This is an opportunity to get the performer's perspective first hand, and to capitalise on that immediate response ensuring that your students get the most our of their time at the theatre.

Scripts
Scripts will be published for each play in a programme format. This provides an opportunity for further study of the text's form and content. Each student has their own copy of each play, at the equivalent of just £1.00. (These texts retail at £6.99).

Discounted Tickets
Tickets are available at the equivalent of just £3 per performance. With tickets normally at £9/£6, this represents a huge discount.

Unbeatable Value
Tickets for shows, scripts for each student, workshops with directors, writers and teachers and aftershow discussions with the company are included in the price. Stage to Page is a pro-active approach to serve mutual needs. An opportunity to tackle your curriculum in a unique, accessible way. Suitable for students of Culture, Theatre Arts, English etc.

What previous participants have said:

"My students don't usually have access to a professional director. It's brilliant"

"This has been the best part of the course for these students...I'm bowled over by the response. Terrific."

"I really got to understand how complicated it is...I was much more into it because I'd read it ...It was great"

For further details or to book please contact Trevelyan Wright, Head of Education on 0121 245 2000

Transmissions

Transmissions: young playwriting

As Birmingham's only venue dedicated entirely to new writing The Door is investing in writers of the future. In Autumn 1998 we ran TRANSMISSIONS 1, with plays written by 7-25 year olds produced as staged readings and performances in The Door. Short plays were developed in primary schools and through the Rep's young people's playwriting groups, led by professional writers and directors. In October 1999 we launched TRANSMISSIONS 2, a year-long project to develop plays by young writers aged 12-25 culminating in a festival of young people's work in July 2,000.

Writing tutors this year are Carl Miller, Noel Greig and Maya Chowdhry

Past success

For TRANSMISSIONS 1 young writers explored speaking, acting and reading one another's work with the guidance of professionals at every stage in the process. They developed their imaginative and technical skills in creating plays with action, speech and character. In December '98 the workshops culminated in a festival of performances. Examples of the extracts and scenes we presented include: *Wish you were here* by Modessor Rashid about a man's past returning to haunt him following his release from prison; Adam Godwin's *The Shop* which centred on the conflict of creativity and responsibility; and *Crossroads* by Sharlene Ferguson in which the friendship between two young women is placed on the line following a night on the town and an unexpected revelation. In all we presented twenty-eight pieces of original writing over a two week period.

"The festival has given me practical tools to write my plays"
Adam Godwin Young Writer

"Helpful encouraging, insightful, inspiring" Tim Jeffries, Young Writer

"Thank you for the chance to work with some inspiring young people"
Maya Chowdhry, Writer

For more information about TRANSMISSIONS please contact; Trevelyan Wright or Caroline Jester on 0121 245 2000

Introducing **The Door**

Since it was founded in 1913 Birmingham Repertory Theatre Company has been a leading national company. Its programming has introduced a range of new and foreign plays to the British theatre repertoire, and it has been a springboard for many internationally famous actors, designers and directors.

As the arts in Birmingham have grown in stature, with the opening of Symphony Hall, the achievements of the city of Birmingham Symphony Orchestra and the arrival of the Birmingham Royal Ballet, so there has been massive investment in the resident theatre company.

Now the company can present classic, new and discovery plays on a scale appropriate to one of the largest acting spaces in Europe, as well as a consistent programme of new theatre in its studio, by some of the brightest contemporary talent. To celebrate this, the space has a new name and a new look.

The Door's programme seeks to find a young and culturally diverse audience for the theatre, through the production of new work in an intimate, flexible space - work, that reflects, defines and enhances their experience of the world while introducing them to the possibilities of the medium.

Twins: Amelda Brown as Mimi and Anne White as Gigi. Photo: Tristram Kenton

Confidence: Jody Watson as Ella, Robin Pirongs as Ben. Photo: Tristram Kenton

Down Red Lane: Matthew Waite as Spider. Photo: Tristram Kenton

Ray Grewal
My Dad's Corner Shop

ff

faber and faber

First published in 2000
by Faber and Faber Limited
3 Queen Square, London WC1N 3AU

Published in the United States by Faber and Faber Inc.
a division of Farrar, Straus and Giroux Inc., New York

Typeset by Country Setting, Kingsdown, Kent CT14 8ES
Printed in England by Intype London Ltd

A CIP record for this book
is available from the British Library

ISBN 0-571-20534-8

2 4 6 8 10 9 7 5 3 1

To our Mother
1937–1988

Characters

Rajesh

Kumar

Old Woman (Grandmother)

Asian Woman (Angel)

Act One

SCENE ONE

Classical Indian music is playing as the lights go up to reveal a corner shop. There is a counter with an old-fashioned till on it and rows of chocolate bars. Next to the till is a little portable radio from which the music is coming. There are shelves with various things stacked on them (canned food, packets of soup, washing powder, pickles etc). There are three doors leading out from the shop: the one on the left opens out into the street, the one behind the till leads to the back of the house and upstairs and the one on the right leads into an alley. It is about 9.30 p.m., half an hour until closing.

Rajesh Sindhu, a twenty-year-old, attractive young man who is quite broad and muscular, is going around the shop pricing items and making sure everything is in the right place. His movements around the shop are fluid, almost dance like.

The door leading into the shop from the street opens and Kumar Sindhu, Rajesh's twenty-three-year-old brother, walks in. He is flamboyantly dressed in a kilt, shin high silver boots, and a tight, lime-green tank top. His hair is done up in two pigtails. He is a young fashion designer, a year out of the London College of Fashion, and he is struggling to make a break in the industry. When he walks in he is carrying his portfolio under one arm and some of his designs in the other. He throws them all to the floor and stands in the centre of the shop, watching his brother. After a moment he storms over to the radio and slams it off.

Rajesh Moody.

Kumar The whole world's crap.

Rajesh They told you to sod off?

Kumar Piss on them. The only way the whole thing could have gotten any worse is if they'd dropped their pants and wiped their arses with my designs. And they thought about it. I could see it in their eyes. Wankers. They're crap, their families are crap and when they have kids they'll probably be crap too. I just don't understand people. (*He assumes a cheesy voice.*) 'Yes, yes, we understand. You're very good, one of the best we've seen. We're always looking to promote new designers, it's our policy, fresh ideas are good ideas. There's definitely promise here.' Then give me a grant you wanker.

Rajesh You're just pissed off 'cause they weren't overwhelmed by your talent.

Kumar Damn flippin' right I'm pissed off. I've got every right to be. Wankers the lot of them.

Rajesh goes into the stockroom through the door behind the counter. Kumar picks up his stuff and dumps it in a corner. Rajesh comes back in carrying a box. He opens it and starts to stack one of the shelves with cheap toilet paper.

Kumar (*a beat*) Has Mum or Dad phoned?

Rajesh Nah, not since last night.

Kumar So Dadiji's probably the same.

Rajesh Probably.

Kumar No news is good news I suppose.

Rajesh Yeah.

Kumar begins to pace around the shop like a restless tiger trapped in its cage.

Kumar Word on the grapevine is that Pierre's gonna do his first big show in a couple of weeks. It's all gonna happen in his mother's flat in Paris.

Rajesh Pierre?

Kumar That French tosser. The one with the moustache like Salvador Dali and the face like a wanker's brother. He was in the year above us at college but he always hung around with us 'cause it made him feel big, that and he was always tryin' to impress the girls with his accent. Shit-head.

Rajesh Sounds like a top bloke.

Kumar A penthouse flat in Paris and apparently anybody who's anybody is gonna be there. And he was crap. He really was, he was terrible. You should have seen his designs. Based on the four seasons and the constellations he used to say. Based on my flippin' hairy 'nads more like. And he's in Paris doing a show. When am I gonna get a break? I'm gettin' older but I ain't gettin' anywhere.

Rajesh You're twenty-three.

Kumar Twenty-three going on twenty-four.

Rajesh Ancient.

Kumar What do you think Lagerfeld, St Laurent or Klein were doin' when they were my age?

Rajesh Tap dancin' for money?

Kumar They were designin' clothes. They were changin' the way people dress. Their couture houses were churnin' out classics like there wasn't any tomorrow. That's what I wanna do. I wanna create something that will withstand the rigors of time, something that people will still be wearing when man meets his maker. Something like crimplene slacks, they've got a half life of fifty million years 'cause they ain't biodegradable, they're gonna be around until the end of time. I wanna create something like that but a lot cooler. When the shit hits the fan and the sun goes nova I want everyone to be puttin' on their favourite design by Kumar Sindhu. It's not too much to ask.

Rajesh I suppose it ain't.

Kumar And once the ball's in motion there's the catwalk shows, the articles by *Vogue*. One day you're in Paris, the next day you're in New York and then you're in Milan. Photographers, celebs, a good dose of super-models, people queuing up to wear something you've made, something you created. And the parties. Can you imagine the kind of parties I'd throw?

Rajesh No.

Kumar Well I can. The music, the champagne, the dancin'. All in some plush hotel room that you trash just before you leave 'cause that's the way things are done.

Rajesh Blah, blah, blah, blah, blah.

Kumar You just don't understand the magic. I need the stress of dealin' with supermodels. You could never let your guard down when you're around them. One minute you're as happy as Larry, the next minute Naomi's in front of you, Cindy's over to your right and Christy's comin' up quickly behind you. Three massive egos flankin' you and it could all be over in a minute.

Rajesh What could?

Kumar The dream. That's the kind of on-the-job training I need, how to deal with a crisis situation. That's the kind of stress that makes you good.

Rajesh You talk such bollocks.

Kumar It ain't bollocks. I can't spend too much longer here. I'm goin' mad, I have to get away. Everything here is so borin'. All of this canned food is sucking the life out of me. I've started to dream about pineapple slices and baked beans. It's the beginning of the end.

Rajesh You should stop dreamin' so much, right, and do some work.

Kumar I was thinkin' about college the other day. I've started to forget things. It's becomin' a vague memory. It was like an oasis in time surrounded by boredom. If I stay here too long I'm gonna forget everything. It's gonna be as if wanting to be a designer was just a dream and now I'm awake and this is it.

Rajesh Good, so do some work.

Kumar My life's in tatters and you want me to stack soup? How can you expect me to do something so mundane when what I should be doin' is goin' out into the big wide world and findin' my focus.

Rajesh You and your flippin' focus. If you want to mess about with clothes all day why don't you stop wasting time and get a job in Kuldip's textile factory?

Kumar Don't toy with me. That's the nub of my problem. I've lost my focus. Those designs over there, they're okay but I know I can do better. I know it. I just have to find my focus again. And it's out there, somewhere, just waitin' for me to stumble across it –

Rajesh (*under his breath*) More chance of stumbling over your own bullshit.

Kumar (*without a pause*) – and when I do, then that'll be it, clothes that will make the world weep and beg for mercy. But instead I'm stuck in here surrounded by Happy Shopper baked beans and cheap bog paper that adheres to your derrière.

Rajesh You should do what Dad says and make do with what you've got instead of moanin' about your focus all the time.

Kumar You be borin' if you want. At least I have an ambition, somethin' to strive for.

Rajesh And I don't?

Kumar Spendin' your life in a corner shop is no ambition.

Rajesh It's a job, ain't it?

Kumar That don't sound like ambition to me. It sounds like acceptin' the obvious.

Rajesh Listen, Suddie came in here this mornin'.

Kumar Suddie?

Rajesh You know, my mate, the one I used to go to school with?

Kumar Oh yeah. What's he done now? Stolen someone's pension?

Rajesh Suddie don't steal anythin'.

Kumar No? But he looks like he could if he wanted to.

Rajesh Anyway, he came in this mornin', right. He was sayin' he'd just come back from one of those adventure holidays. He'd been sailin', orienteerin', sleepin' in a tent, that kind of stuff. One of the days they went canoein' down some river. It was really rough, he said, and he'd smashed his arm against a rock. Really buggered it up. Broke it in about three hundred different places and now he has no feelin' in his right hand. Nothing. And the doctors say that's probably the way it's gonna stay for the rest of his life.

A pause.

Kumar Thanks for sharing that with me. I'll take it to the grave.

Rajesh You're too westernised. All you think about is leavin' here, leavin' Mum and Dad.

Kumar Oh, don't give me that shit.

Rajesh It's true, right. You don't do anything they ask you to and every time they try to talk to you about gettin' married you just ignore them.

Kumar Of course I ignore them, as if I'm gettin' married when I don't even have a proper job. Anyway, I hate to think what kind of woman they'd want me to meet.

Rajesh That last one wasn't too bad.

Kumar Oh please, she had all the allure of road kill.

Rajesh I would have met her.

Kumar That's 'cause you're soft.

Rajesh Oh right, as if I'm gonna worry about crap like findin' myself someone when every week Mum and Dad come up with someone new for me to meet. Why should I worry about it when they are? As soon as they find me a girl with good child-bearin' facilities, right, I'll say yeah.

Kumar Big arse and big tits?

Rajesh I'm a simple man with simple needs. And as long as she can make rotis that are just slightly burnt and crispy and aloo gobi the way I like it, I'll be happy.

Kumar And love has nothing to do with it?

Rajesh Love shmuv. I'd rather have a woman who keeps the house clean and looks after the kids than someone who keeps stickin' her tongue in my ear.

Kumar Well I ain't like you. I want to find my own woman. Not one of these girls who do exactly what their parents say. I want someone who wants to see the world with me. Someone who likes a bit of adventure. Someone who I can talk to about stuff that's important. And someone I can get totally pissed with and not feel guilty or embarrassed. Shit knows where I'm gonna find her.

Rajesh Probably standin' next to your focus.

Kumar Oh har dee har har.

Rajesh Anyway, I thought you were goin' out with someone. Terry said he saw you in town with a woman.

Kumar I ain't seein' anyone. And tell Terry to keep his nose out of my arse.

Rajesh Well, look at these girl-friends you've had before, right, what the hell has ever come of it?

Kumar Life experience.

Rajesh Bollocks, you just get miserable.

Kumar (*thoughtfully*) No one ever said all life experience is good experience. (*Pause.*) And don't call me westernised like it's a bad thing and I'm the only one that is. You're westernised, Mum and Dad are westernised and so's everyone else who came to this country. If they didn't want to be westernised they wouldn't have come here; they had a choice. But now all the mums and dads are lookin' at their kids and seein' that they have aspirations, and dreams, and ambitions that they never had when they were young. And it scares them. Scares them that their kids wanna be somethin' different, wanna be somethin' more than they could ever be. So they look at you with their beady eyes and they tell you you're too westernised like you've got a disease. Okay, I can live with that. I can live with havin' a dream.

Rajesh Fine. And I'll stay with Mum and Dad when they're old.

Kumar Good for you. That means I don't have to, and seein' as you're the youngest son it's your duty to stay with them.

Rajesh I don't mind, I like it here.

Kumar You're mad. This place is crap.

Rajesh Ever since you came back all you've done is complain, right. You never give it a chance. You don't even try to get to know the people who come in here every day. They ask for somethin', right, and you give them an answer like they're stupid for askin' in the first place and you'd rather be doin' somethin' else. When Dad asks you to help with the books you piss about until he has to do them himself and when Mum asks you to help her change the stuff in the window you act as if she wants to kill your first born, and then she feels guilty and does it herself. You think everything you do is so important, right, when really it's bollocks and no one around here cares. Maybe when you tell your arty mates that you've got some of Annie Leibovitz's snot in a jar they jump half way to the moon but every normal person thinks who the shit is Annie Leibovitz? And it's not because they're stupid, right, it's because they don't care. Crap like that doesn't matter, Ku. What matters is keepin' these shelves stocked so when people come in in the mornin' they can get what they want. Keepin' the books right matters so we've all got some money at the end of the week. And keepin' the shop open matters 'cause Dad struggled for years in a factory doin' what he was told, right, but now this is his and he does what he wants. This is our shop. We own it. That's what matters.

Kumar I take it you're not gonna be too impressed if I tell you I saw the back of Kate Moss's head this afternoon?

Rajesh gives up on his brother and goes back to stacking the shelf.

I know the shop's important. I used to help Dad at the cash and carry when you were still wearin' nappies, it's just that I can't get excited about stackin' cheap bog roll.

Rajesh Why does it have to be excitin'? Why don't you just do it?

Kumar It has to be excitin' otherwise it just numbs your brain.

Kumar goes over to where Rajesh is stacking the shelf and begins to play with a roll of toilet tissue.

I don't know, maybe the challenge is makin' bog roll aesthetically pleasin'? Where's the poetry, the mystery in bog roll? Maybe those are the kind of questions I should be askin' myself? When is bog roll not bog roll? Is there more here than simply meets the eye? Whose arse did this paper clean before it was recycled? But maybe there's something in that, the fact that it's recycled. What do you think that's a metaphor for?

Rajesh What are you talkin' about?

Kumar Who thinks about where bog roll comes from or goes to. This roll of paper probably goes on some epic journey from the cheeks of one person to the cheeks of someone else. What have you seen, bog roll, that I haven't?

Rajesh The inside of someone's arse.

Kumar Where have you been that I will never go? What have you felt that I can never feel?

Kumar hugs the toilet tissue. Rajesh shakes his head.

I'm beginnin' to think I could do somethin' with this. Maybe we should clear this whole wall. Dedicate the whole thing to toilet rolls. Make it into a sort of cycle, maybe into a sort of shrine. Hindus and Sikhs believe that you live so many lives before you go to heaven. Maybe for bog roll, heaven is being turned into a book to be studied for ever instead of being flushed away constantly. Come on, help me clear this whole wall.

Rajesh snatches the toilet tissue off him and puts it back on the shelf.

Rajesh Dick.

Kumar looks dejected; he really was getting into it. Rajesh goes into the back room. Kumar goes over to his bag and takes some fliers for Miss Moneypenny's out of it. He goes over to the till and starts to make a nice display with them. Rajesh returns a moment later with a box of canned soup.

Will you stop cluttering up the till with that crap, no one ever takes one.

Kumar Some day someone will and I'll feel as if I've achieved something.

Rajesh Miss Moneypenny's? What the hell's that? Night-clubs are stupid.

Kumar You've never been to one, so what do you know? Nightclubs are magical, mysterious places, full of wonder, where anything can happen and most times does.

Rajesh Bollocks. (*He kneels down and rips open the box.*) Mr Mittar came by this afternoon.

Kumar You mean Dad's spy.

Rajesh He came to drop off the stock, which took ten minutes, right, and then he spent two hours telling me about his ingrowing toe nails, his sore back, his grey hair and the fact that Mrs Mittar won't let him sleep in their bed any more 'cause his fartin' keeps her awake. And then he spent another hour tellin' me that the pavement outside his house was sinkin' and he was goin' to the council to complain. I was this far away (*indicating with his fingers*) from punchin' his lights out 'cause he was drivin' me nuts.

Kumar We don't order as much from the cash and carry as we used to, do we?

Rajesh (*putting two cans on the shelf*) No, probably not.

Kumar And it don't take you that long to fill the shelves any more.

Rajesh Whatever, watch this. There's twenty-two cans in here, right. I bet I can lift it over my head at least a hundred times.

Kumar Amazin'.

Rajesh (*lifting the cans over his head*) One, two, three, four.

Kumar Ironic isn't it?

Rajesh Seven, eight. Yeah. Nine, ten.

Kumar What?

Rajesh Eleven, twelve. Whatever it is, I'm sure it's the most ironic thing. Thirteen, fourteen.

Kumar You don't even know what I'm talkin' about.

Rajesh No and I don't care. Sixteen, seventeen.

Kumar I was gonna tell you somethin' important.

Rajesh No you weren't. Twenty, twenty-one. Maybe with your arty mates you can start a conversation with 'Ironic isn't it,' but not with me. Twenty-four, twenty-five.

Kumar Well, it is ironic.

Rajesh Probably. Twenty-nine, thirty, thirty-one, thirty-two, thirty-three, thirty-four, thirty-five, thirty-six, thirty-

Kumar I was just gonna say that it's ironic that we own a shop but we still do all our shoppin' at the Co-op.

Rajesh You're right, that's ironic. It's probably the most ironic thing I've heard all day. Forty, forty-one.

Kumar I think we're gonna have to close the shop soon.

Rajesh Bollocks. Forty-four, forty-five.

Kumar We sell everything dearer then the supermarket. And now the supermarket stays open longer than we do. They sell more things and have a wider variety. And if I had the choice, even I'd rather go there.

Rajesh You would. Fifty-nine, sixty. The shop ain't gonna close. People still come in here.

Kumar But not as many as used to. Even I've noticed that.

Rajesh People always forget things. That's why they need the corner shop. For the things they don't remember when they go shoppin'. Or when they run out. Sixty-three, sixty-four.

Kumar That isn't enough to keep the shop open. Before I went to college people used to come in here and do their shoppin'. Now they come in and buy a Mars bar or a can of beans. The shop can't stay open if only three people come in here in a day and they all buy a loaf of bread each. (*He walks over to the till.*) We'll just have to keep on puttin' up the prices and then people won't come here at all. I mean, look how much we've taken today.

*Kumar presses a button and the till shoots open.
Rajesh drops the box of soup cans and marches over
to the counter. He slams the till shut.*

Rajesh What the hell are you talkin' about? It's not as
if you do anything around here, right, so how come
suddenly you're an expert? I do the books and I know
we're doin' okay. People are always gonna use this shop.

Kumar That Singh's shop on Howell Street, that's closed
now.

Rajesh 'Cause he didn't know what he was doin', right?

Kumar I'm just sayin', I think the days of the corner
shop are numbered.

Rajesh The only time you ever talk about the shop,
right, is to say something stupid like that. You don't help
out, you don't do anything, but as soon as there's some
bad news to talk about then you're the first one to start
chattin'.

Kumar I was just sayin' it was ironic.

Rajesh Bollocks to ironic. Either do some work or shut
up and play with your pictures.

Kumar Bollocks to you.

*Rajesh starts to tidy up. As he passes the counter he
grabs the fliers for Miss Moneypenny's in one hand
and throws them into the bin beside the counter.
Kumar takes a step towards him. Then stops. An
uncomfortable silence.*

*The door leading into the shop opens and an Old
Indian Woman walks in. She is dressed very
traditionally and there is an other-worldly air about
her. She seems bemused, amazed and bewildered by
everything around her.*

*When the Old Woman's eyes settle on the two
brothers she starts to cry.*

Old Woman (*with a broad Indian accent*) God, I have
prayed for this day for so long.

*She shuffles over to Kumar. First she runs a hand over
his cheek and then she throws her arms around him.
Kumar looks decidedly uncomfortable.*

Caca, are you Kumar? I have spent many years yearning
to look into your eyes, yearning to see your face. You are
my son and I have a very special gift for you. Come
outside with me and I will share it with you.

An expression of terror on Kumar's face.

Kumar No, I'm not Kumar, I'm Rajesh. (*nodding at
Rajesh*) He's Kumar.

*Rajesh throws him a disapproving look as the Old
Woman disengages herself from Kumar with obvious
disgust and starts to shuffle towards him. But before
she can get to him off-stage the phone begins to ring.
The two brothers look at each other.*

You answer it.

Rajesh What about her?

Kumar I'll deal with her.

*Rajesh goes into the back room and answers the
phone. The Old Woman tries to follow him.*

(*taking her arm*) No auntyji, you can't go back there.

Old Woman But I must see Kumar, I must. I have something for him.

Kumar leads her towards the door.

Kumar I'm sure whatever it is he can live without it.

Old Woman Caca, I have come a long way to see him, I am risking the greatest punishment. What I have is something he might desire.

Kumar Oh gross. Auntyji, you lost what he desires a long, long, long, *long* time ago. (*He opens the door.*) Now why don't you go back to lala land where I'm sure there are loads of men who want what you have.

Old Woman But they told me I do not have much time. (*She grabs hold of one of the shelves.*) Caca, do you have no respect? How can you abuse me this way? I am going nowhere until I have spoken to him.

Kumar Oh God.

He gently pulls her away from the shelf. As he pushes her out of the door the Old Woman grabs arm fulls of anything that she can lay her hands on hoping that he won't kick her out if she has some of his merchandise. Kumar keeps pushing her regardless.

Why don't you come back in the morning, we're open to nutcases between ten and eleven.

Kumar leads the Old Woman outside. Before he can close the door we hear the Old Woman . . .

Old Woman (*off-stage*) Kumar, let me be your inspiration!

Kumar closes the door as Rajesh comes back into the shop.

Kumar Well?

Rajesh It was Dad. He said Mum's ill. It's nothing serious just the water's a bit dodgy. He was sayin' that most of our aunts and uncles are there now, there's about thirty of them stuck in one house drivin' each other crazy.

Kumar What about Dadiji?

Rajesh She's still the same. She can't move. Can't talk. She can't even eat any more. They don't think she's got that long. Maybe just a day or two.

A pause.

Kumar It's mad to think that one day everythin' ends. I hope that when it's my turn and I'm lyin' there I can look back and think I did everything that I wanted to do, I experienced everythin' I could. (*Beat.*) I'm goin' to bed.

He collects his portfolio and designs, and leaves. We hear him run up the stairs. Rajesh makes sure the door leading into the shop is locked and then he picks the empty boxes up off the floor. He goes to the door that leads out into the alley. He takes a big bunch of keys out of his pocket and unlocks it. He opens it and steps outside. We hear him open a wheelie bin and start to throw the rubbish into it.
It is then that the low rumbling sound starts. It grows steadily louder until it seems to shake the stage.
Suddenly a brilliant bright white light pours in through the open door.

Rajesh (*off-stage*) OH SHIT!!!

The lights go out.

SCENE TWO

Morning, around eight thirty, and the shop is empty and silent . . . until Kumar stumbles in through the door that leads into the rest of the house. He is half dressed, half asleep and suffering from severe bed-head. He is carrying a mug of coffee which he puts onto the counter. He takes a Flake from the chocolate bar rack. He is about to peel off the wrapper when he finally notices that Rajesh is not around.

Kumar Raj?!

No answer.

Raj?!!

No answer.

RAJ???!!!!!!

Still no answer.

Where the hell is he? (*Beat.*) I see what he's doin', tryin' to teach me a lesson, leavin' me here alone to do all the work. Git. (*He raises his voice slightly, thinking Rajesh is hidden away somewhere nearby.*) Well I'll teach you a lesson. I ain't gonna open the stupid shop, then we'll see who's learnt what. Think you're so flippin' clever, well I'm the one who went to college.

Kumar leans against the counter and opens the Flake. He takes a bite and chews slowly. He starts to tap his feet. He is about to take another bite but he snaps.

Bollocks!

He marches over to the door. He unlocks it and switches the sign from CLOSED *to* OPEN. *As he is doing this the door leading out into the alley creaks open and Rajesh drifts in like an apparition. His clothes are in total disarray. His skin has a pale bleached look to it and his hair is sticking out all over the place.*

(*without turning*) Where the shit have you been? (*turning*) Oh, great hair. Paul Mitchell?

Rajesh (*very quietly*) Leave me alone.

Kumar What is it? Are you sick?

Rajesh I . . .

He staggers, almost falls. Kumar rushes over to him and puts an arm around his waist.

Kumar Shit. What the flippin' hell happened?

Rajesh . . . sit down.

Kumar helps him over to a chair. Rajesh collapses into it with obvious relief. He rests his head in his hands, all the time shaking it slowly.

Kumar What is it? What happened? Did someone beat you up? Were you mugged? Did you pass out in the alley? Did you sleep there all night? Is it a tumour? Did you haemorrhage? Are you bleeding internally? Christ, how do I deal with this? Where do I stick the band aid? Can you hold on a minute while I have another cup of coffee, get my head together? I'm all over the place.

Rajesh Will you shut up!

Silence for a moment.

Kumar Well?

Rajesh Well what?

Kumar What happened?

Rajesh It's . . . hard to explain.

Kumar Why? What did you do? You didn't shoot up did you? 'Cause that ain't chic. Some people think it is, but it ain't.

Rajesh 'Cause I didn't.

Kumar Then what?

Rajesh It's nothin'.

Kumar What do you mean, it's nothin'? Obviously it's somethin'.

Rajesh Maybe I just dreamt it.

Kumar Dreamt what?

Rajesh You know those really vivid dreams you have sometimes, when the maddest things are happenin' but no matter how mad they are they seem real?

Kumar Yeah, I know.

Rajesh Well maybe it was like that. Just a vivid dream.

Kumar What? Maybe what was like that?

Rajesh It's just so hard to believe.

Kumar You either tell me what happened or I'm gonna rip your tits off.

Rajesh Last night, when you went to bed, I was closing the shop, right. I got together all the crap that was lyin' around and I went outside to the bins.

Kumar Yeaaah.

Rajesh And suddenly there was this noise.

Kumar A noise?

Rajesh This sound, right. Like thunder really far away.

Kumar Thunder? Lightnin'?

Rajesh It wasn't thunder, it was like thunder. And then there was this light, right. Really bright.

Kumar Like a headlight?

Rajesh Nah.

Kumar Like a torch?

Rajesh No.

Kumar Maybe the police helicopter, they've got a spot-light they're always shinin' around.

Rajesh I don't think so.

Kumar What then? God?

Rajesh Welll . . .

Kumar God?

Rajesh Well, sort of.

Kumar What? You saw God?

Rajesh Not God exactly. More alien . . . y.

Kumar What the hell are you talkin' about?

Rajesh Last night when I was throwin' the rubbish out I was . . . I was abducted by aliens.

Kumar's jaw drops.

Kumar You were abducted by aliens?

Rajesh That's what happened, right.

Kumar Aliens?

Rajesh Yeah.

Kumar Beings from another world?

Rajesh I'm tryin' to come to terms with it myself.

Kumar I don't believe it.

Rajesh How do you think I feel?

Kumar I don't believe it.

Rajesh You've gotta believe me. That's what happened.

Kumar I flippin' don't believe it. Why the hell did they abduct you? Why didn't they abduct me? I would have appreciated it more.

Rajesh Oh God. Leave me alone.

Kumar Leave you alone? What the hell are you talkin' about? Give me all the details.

Rajesh I can't really remember that much.

Kumar Weren't you makin' notes?

Rajesh As a matter of fact, no.

Kumar What did they look like?

Rajesh All I could see was shadows.

Kumar Well did they look like E.T. or were they more like the Blob?

Rajesh I couldn't really tell.

Kumar Did they have eyes or did they use some weird kind of sensory perception?

Rajesh I don't know.

Kumar Did you try to communicate with them? I mean, if it was me I'd have had flippin' loads of questions to ask them. They wouldn't have been able to shut me up. I mean if they wear clothes what kind of fabrics do they use? Is it some kind of hi-tech synthetic stuff that repels dust or are there alien sheep?

Rajesh Sorry, I forgot to ask.

Kumar Then were you probed? At least tell me they stuck somethin' in you?

Rajesh No I wasn't.

Kumar No soreness?

Rajesh Piss off.

Kumar Well, that was all a bit anticlimactic wasn't it? You didn't see anything, you can't remember anythin' and you weren't even probed. Only you could make an alien abduction sound that borin'.

Rajesh There is somethin'.

Kumar What? How much more uninteresting can you make this?

Rajesh I can see things.

Kumar Things? What things?

Rajesh Images. Drawings, I think. In my head.

Kumar Images of what?

Rajesh I don't know. Lots of lines and shapes. They seem to be floatin' in front of me, in my head. Some come into focus, right, and others become blurred. Then they swap around.

Kumar Put there by the aliens?

Rajesh Yeah.

Kumar Wow. Let's get them out.

Rajesh What?

Kumar Draw them.

Kumar rushes over to the counter and takes a pen and a pad from behind it. He then goes back to Rajesh and hands them to him.

Go on.

Rajesh I don't know if I can, you know I'm crap at drawin'.

Kumar Try.

Rajesh starts to scribble on the pad. Kumar looks over his shoulder. At first Rajesh is hesitant but as the drawing takes shape his strokes become more confident and purposeful until he proudly presents the completed picture to Kumar.

Rajesh Well, what is it?

Kumar turns the drawing over and over in his hands.

Is it a star chart or somethin'? Is it the plans to . . . I dunno, some kind of machine. Some complex somethin', right, that could maybe effect the way we live? Maybe it's a car that runs off air. Do you think? I mean it could be anythin'.

Kumar It's the pattern for a dress.

Rajesh What!?

Kumar An evening dress. Slightly off the shoulder with a really low back. It hints at Donna Karan and nods at Vivienne Westwood but it's more. Much more. Oh my God. Quick draw another one.

Rajesh takes the pad and draws another image onto it. Before he has even finished Kumar snatches it off him. Kumar looks at the sketch and swoons as if he is about to faint. He clutches one of the shelves.

Oh God. This is it.

Rajesh This is what?

Kumar My focus. This is my focus. No wonder I couldn't find it – it was on another planet.

Rajesh Give that here.

He snatches the drawings back off Kumar.

What the hell are you talkin' about, dresses? They have to be somethin' else. They have to be.

Kumar (*snatching them back*) They are somethin' else, they're amazin'. If I start with this, and whatever else is in your head, then I could go anywhere, I could do anythin'. Maybe somethin' in silk, maybe somethin' in velvet. And polynovix. Oh God lots of polynovix. The possibilities. I'm beginnin' to see it. It's becomin' clear. A whole line of evening wear. For women but especially for men. A fashion revolution. Everything has become too retrospective. The look of the future. Somethin' so different and yet so obviously simple. Poetry. Are you listenin'? This is poetry.

Rajesh (*snatching them back*) You're talkin' bollocks.

Kumar It's the truth.

Rajesh Crap. I know what you're doin'. You can't stick it that the aliens chose me, it's really buggin' you that they didn't take you, isn't it?

Kumar What? What are you talkin' about?

Rajesh Well, they did choose me. I ain't so boring no more. I'm the one who can phone up my mates and say guess what happened to me last night, not you. I'm suddenly the one who's special, right. So maybe I should go out and collect some celebrity snot or prance about like a fanny and talk shite like how puce is the new orange.

Kumar Brown was the new black, you bumbrain.

Rajesh Whatever.

Kumar You can do whatever you want, I don't care, just let me see the drawin's.

Rajesh No.

Kumar Why?

Rajesh 'Cause they're mine.

Kumar What? It's my focus.

Rajesh My drawin's; my focus.

Kumar Your focus?! You don't have a focus, fanny-face.

Rajesh I do now, Mr arty-farty man. The aliens chose me so the images must have somethin' to do with . . . the shop.

Kumar What?!

Rajesh 'Course. (*He examines the drawings.*) I see it now. Plans to make the corner shop the best in the world. Motion sensitive automatic doors. Hi-tech consumer friendly tills. Bar-code readin' portable price packs. (*touching his head*) Another one coming into focus. Remote controlled shoppin' trolleys!

Kumar Those things already exist, shit-head (except for maybe the last one, that's a fab idea). Show me the drawings.

Rajesh No.

Kumar tries to get them off him. Rajesh holds them above his head and keeps batting away Kumar's hands.

Kumar Show me.

Rajesh No, Mr I-think-we're-gonna-have-to-close-the-shop. Not any more we're not.

Kumar Let me see.

Rajesh No.

Kumar Come on, you arse.

Rajesh No.

Kumar gives Rajesh a shove.

Kumar Let me see them you twat.

Rajesh, angry now, grabs one of Kumar's arms and pins it behind his back. Kumar moans in pain and tries to struggle free but Rajesh kicks his legs out from under him and, once he has Kumar on the floor, he sits on him still pinning his arm behind his back. With his free hand Rajesh playfully slaps the back of his brother's head.

Rajesh They're my images, I'll do whatever I want with them. You don't have a say 'cause it's none of your business. The aliens chose me.

After a moment torturing his brother, Rajesh lets Kumar get to his feet.

Kumar Show me the drawin's.

Rajesh No.

Kumar pushes past him and disappears into the back of the house.

The door leading into the corner shop opens and the Old Woman walks in. She seems a lot more composed than she was yesterday. She goes over to a shelf and picks up a box of Tampons and takes them to the counter and waits to be served.

Rajesh has no choice, he has to serve her. He walks behind the counter.

Old Woman Hello, how is your health this morning?

Rajesh It's okay.

Old Woman Good, good. Tell me, are you still designing suits?

Rajesh What?

Old Woman Are you still drawing?

Rajesh Drawin'? I might be.

Old Woman Have you . . . been inspired?

Rajesh Maybe. Auntyji, who are you?

Old Woman No one. All is well. Your father told me you were unhappy, if that has passed then I am glad.

Keep hope. One day people will want to see the clothes you make.

Rajesh Clothes? I don't make clothes. Kumar does.

Old Woman But yesterday you said you were Kumar.

Rajesh My brother's an idiot, he was messin' about.

Old Woman But then that must mean you are Rajesh?

Rajesh Yeah.

Old Woman Obedient, loyal Rajesh?

Rajesh I suppose.

Old Woman Rajesh who never puts a foot wrong. Rajesh who respects and honours his parents?

Rajesh I guess.

Old Woman Rajesh, who believes a woman's place is in the home?

Rajesh I've never really thought about it, but – you know . . .

Old Woman Rajesh who would quash a woman's spirit before she had grown?

Rajesh That's not fair.

Old Woman Rajesh who, no doubt, has never been with a woman.

Rajesh What?!! Auntyji, that's none of your bloody business. Now do you want those Tampons or not?

Old Woman No. I was hoping you were different, I was hoping things had changed. All is lost. (*She walks towards the door. Mumbling to herself*) Just like his father. And his father before him.

The Old Woman leaves. Rajesh is left alone and confused by all that has just happened.

34

SCENE THREE

*Late afternoon and Rajesh is standing behind the
counter. He is leaning against it and scribbling away on a
piece of paper as he composes a letter. Kumar is sitting
in a corner as far away from his brother as he can get.
He has his sketch pad resting on his lap and he is trying
to come up with some new designs.*

*To wind Kumar up, Rajesh is reading the letter out
loud as he writes it.*

Rajesh Dear Stephen Hawking, the other day when I
was throwing out the rubbish. (*Beat. He scribbles out
the line and starts again.*) Dear Stephen Hawking, the
other day whilst I was throwing out the rubbish. (*He
stops and scribbles out the line.*) Dear Doctor Hawking,
the other day whilst I was d-i-s-pos-ing of the g-ar-b-age.

Kumar What the hell are you doin', you idiot?

Rajesh Writing a letter.

Kumar Talkin' shite more like.

Rajesh I've been thinkin'.

Kumar I thought I could smell somethin'.

Rajesh I've been thinkin', right, that maybe the images
in my head aren't the blueprints for corner-shop-related
accessories.

Kumar (*sarcastically*) No.

Rajesh I mean realistically, right, the aliens probably had
to travel a couple of hundred light years to get here so
obviously they're cleverer than we are. So if they're
cleverer they're more advanced. If they're more advanced
they have better computers. If they have better computers
they've got a bigger internet system and they've got a

wider variety of on-line shopping networks. If they've got a wider variety of on-line shopping networks they obvious don't have corner shops.

Kumar You are so stupid it makes me want to cry.

Rajesh So if the images haven't got anythin' to do with the shop what are they?

Kumar Patterns for clothes.

Rajesh Blueprints for machines that are gonna change the way we live our lives.

Kumar They're patterns for dresses, bum head.

Rajesh So what I'm gonna do, right, is draw some of the images and send them to the greatest scientists around the world.

Kumar Stephen Hawking is not gonna look good in a knee-length satin cocktail dress.

Rajesh And let them make the machines.

Kumar Let them laugh at the idiot who thought that preliminary sketches for a range of evenin' wear were the blueprints for solar energy generators.

Rajesh But I'm gonna do the whole thing anonymously, right. My plan is to let them figure out what the machines do and worry about buildin' them. And, okay, they'll probably take the credit, right, but as the world is slowly transformed into . . . a . . . better place to be and we get rid of war and pollution and all sorts of other crap stuff that we could do without I'm gonna write it all down in a diary. I'm gonna watch the world become the kind of place we all dream about it being. And all the while I'm gonna keep this diary. And then, just before I die, right, I'm gonna have it published. I'll call it something like 'Me and the aliens . . . and the night

I was takin' out the rubbish . . . and how that changed the world for ever,' by Rajesh Sindhu.

Kumar Subtle title.

Rajesh And just as I'm about to pop my cork the whole world is gonna realise what a top bloke I was. And the shop will probably become a place of pilgrimage after I'm dead.

Kumar Sounds as if you've got it all figured out.

Rajesh Yeah.

Kumar I'll probably be remembered as the brother of the greatest man who ever lived.

Rajesh Yeah, probably.

Kumar You're a shithead.

Kumar goes back to his sketches and Rajesh goes back to his letter.

Rajesh Dear Doctor Hawking, the other night whilst disposing of the . . . refuse, I encountered visitors from another world. Although I neither saw, felt nor heard them I know they were from another planet because they shone a bright light at me and then took me to their spaceship. At least, I am assuming they took me to their spaceship because I didn't see that either. But I spent the night lying on a cold, hard surface that could only have been an examination table staring into a bright light. Don't worry, Doctor Hawking, this isn't another crazy abduction and then getting probed story because they didn't do that either. And now that I think about it the cold, hard surface could have been the pavement and the bright light could have been from the old street lights we still have in the alley. (*He pauses.*) But, Doctor Hawking, I am sure right now you are asking yourself the same question I am: why would I spend the whole night lying outside on the pavement?

Kumar 'Cause you're an idiot.

Rajesh begins to tap his pen against the counter thoughtfully.

Rajesh Do you believe in aliens?

Kumar Yeah.

Rajesh I mean really.

Kumar Yeah.

Rajesh Seriously.

Kumar Yes!

Rajesh I've been thinkin'.

Kumar Again? Wait while I call the *Guinness Book of Records*.

Rajesh Maybe I wasn't abducted by aliens.

Kumar Why?

Rajesh I don't believe in aliens.

Kumar Just because you don't believe in them doesn't mean they don't exist. You didn't believe there was such a thing as the Prince Albert until I showed you that picture.

Rajesh Thanks for reminding me. But this is different, right. Creatures from another world. It's just crazy talk.

Kumar You were abducted by aliens, accept it. You've become a member of an exclusive society populated mainly by red-neck Americans who marry their own sisters.

Rajesh That's exactly it. You've got to be crazy to believe in aliens and I ain't crazy.

Kumar No, you're just borin', but there's no law sayin' strange things can't happen to borin' people.

Rajesh It couldn't have been aliens. Stephen Hawking probably doesn't believe in aliens and he knows a lot of stuff about a lot of stuff, right?

Kumar Stephen Hawking is an alien. Ask anybody who's ever read his book whether they understood it? I bet they say no. Only people from his home planet know what he's babblin' on about.

Rajesh Nah, it weren't aliens.

Kumar Then what was it?

Rajesh I don't know.

Kumar Bright lights, weird sensation, strange images. That's like the ABC of alien abduction.

Rajesh Maybe I just passed out, maybe I fainted, fell over, knocked my head and that was it. Or maybe something hit me on the head, right, rubbish from a plane, a tile fallin' off the roof, or even a dead bird?

Kumar A dead bird?

Rajesh Birds die, don't they?

Kumar In mid-flight?

Rajesh I'm just sayin' it could happen.

Kumar Then how do you explain the images?

Rajesh Too much time spent listenin' to your bollocks.

Kumar So you listen to me and then one mornin' you wake up and you're Coco flippin' Chanel?

Rajesh I'm just tryin' to be realistic.

Kumar So you weren't abducted by aliens?

Rajesh No.

Kumar And the images in your head aren't the blueprints for machines that are gonna change mankind?

Rajesh No.

Kumar Then draw some and show them to me.

Rajesh No.

Kumar Why?

Rajesh It's best if we just forget the whole thing.

Kumar You have my focus in your head and you want me to forget the whole thing?

Rajesh Yeah, just forget I ever mentioned it.

He picks up the letter, screws it up and throws it into a small bin beside the counter.

The world ain't such a bad place, right, and who knows changing it might just make it worse. Change ain't always a good thing.

Kumar Just draw a couple of sketches.

Rajesh Forget it. Dad's always tellin' us to make do with what we have so you make do with what you've got and I'll make do with what I've got.

Kumar But outside of havin' my focus you ain't got anythin', you idiot.

Rajesh I've got my health and the shop.

Kumar Just draw one sketch, just one.

Rajesh No.

Kumar Why?

Rajesh 'Cause it never happened.

Kumar It should have happened to me you brainless git.

Rajesh But it didn't. It didn't happen at all.

Kumar You're not even gonna give me one sketch?

Rajesh Forget it.

Kumar Shithead!!

The door leading into the shop from the street opens and the Old Woman pokes her head in. She seems satisfied with what she sees so she promptly leaves.

Great, the crazies are coming out of the woodwork again.

He gets up and walks over to the back door.

Rajesh Where you goin'?

Kumar Somewhere where I can think.

He leaves. Just as the door swings shut behind him the door leading out into the street bursts open and the Old Woman walks in. But this time she is not alone. She is dragging a young Asian Woman with her. The Asian Woman is in her late twenties and is dressed in a pure white salwar khamiz.
Rajesh looks at her . . . and is enchanted.
The Asian Woman clearly does not want to be here.
The two women move to the front of the stage and argue in hushed voices. Rajesh remains behind the counter clearly wanting to approach the Asian Woman but hindered by his own inhibitions. He begins to mangle some of the chocolate bars as he goes through the turmoil of deciding whether or not to talk to her.

Asian Woman (*a strange neutral accent as though she is from nowhere*) Well, where's the other one?

Old Woman He was here a moment ago.

Asian Woman Well, he's not here now.

Old Woman That is hardly my fault.

Asian Woman We should not be doing this.

Old Woman We must.

Asian Woman But this is almost a crime. I could lose my job.

Old Woman Job, shmob. We must at least try to put things right. Rajesh will never accept what we have given him. He will loathe it and reject it. He's a fool like all men. Only Kumar is different.

Asian Woman I asked you if it was the right brother, how could you get them mixed up?

Old Woman They lied to me.

Asian Woman I knew I shouldn't have listened to you. Essence transference is something you have to think about, not something you can rush into. I was a fool to agree to it, a fool. And to think I made such an awful mistake, me! Not in a million millennia have I ever made a mistake. Oh the shame, the ignominy.

Old Woman Do not be too hard on yourself, it was partly my fault.

Asian Woman Partly!

Finally Rajesh leaves the counter and heads towards them.

Old Woman Quickly, pretend to be buying something.

The Old Woman takes a tub of mixed pickles off the shelf and slaps it into the Asian Woman's hand. The Asian Woman holds the tub at arm's length; there is a look of revulsion on her face.

Rajesh (*nervously*) N . . . need any help.

Old Woman Not from an oppressor of women.

Rajesh Auntyji, I've never oppressed anyone.

Old Woman Probably not from want of trying.

Rajesh I don't know who you've been talkin' to –

Old Woman I don't need to be told what I can see with my own eyes.

Rajesh All I wanted to know was whether your grand-daughter had the right pickle?

Old Woman She isn't my grand-daughter.

Rajesh She isn't?

Rajesh turns to the Asian Woman and opens his mouth as if he is about to say something. After a moment he closes it and seems to slump physically.

We have an offer on, buy one get two free – I mean, buy two get one free.

He heads back to the counter. The Asian Woman drops the pickle.

Asian Woman How repugnant is everything in this place! Everything smells, everything is dirty, even the air is like a thick smoke. I don't want to be here a moment longer than I must.

Old Woman How long do we have?

Asian Woman Two days, as soon as your body dies we must go. But I cannot stand the thought of being here for so long.

Old Woman Quickly then, what shall we do?

Asian Woman There is only one thing to do, I must take your essence from this brother, return it to you, then we must go and find Kumar.

Old Woman Perfect. Hurry then.

The Asian Woman takes a step towards Rajesh. And then stops.

Old Woman What is it?

Asian Woman To take your essence from him I must place my lips against his.

Old Woman Yes?

Asian Woman I have never touched a man's lips before and to be completely honest I find the prospect acutely abhorrent.

Old Woman Just close your eyes and think of something else.

Asian Woman Like what, for instance?

Old Woman Like swimming in a clear blue sea. That is what I used to do all the time.

Asian Woman I have never swum in a clear blue sea.

Old Woman Oh God. Then think of anything. Our time here grows shorter by the minute while you stand around worrying about foolish things.

The Asian Woman turns back to Rajesh. After a moment she turns back to the Old Woman.

Asian Woman He's staring at me. I cannot do it while he's staring at me.

Old Woman What does it matter?

Asian Woman We cannot reveal ourselves to him. People are notoriously thick-headed when it comes to spiritual matters. If he were to discover our true identities he might become a gibbering wreck. I've seen it happen before. Distract him.

The Old Woman lets out an exasperated sigh. She takes two tubs of pickles off the shelf and walks over to the counter.

Old Woman Rajesh, which of these pickles is the hottest?

Rajesh I ain't got the faintest idea.

Old Woman Then can you find out?

Rajesh And how'm I supposed to do that?

Old Woman Open them, let me taste them.

Rajesh I can't open them unless you want to buy them.

Old Woman I cannot buy one unless I know which one I want.

Rajesh It usually says on the label.

Rajesh takes the pickles and inspects the labels. All this time the Asian Woman is sneaking up behind him. She pauses. The Old Woman indicates for her to hurry.

I think –

He gets no further. The Asian Woman taps him on the shoulder. Rajesh turns. The Asian Woman grabs his head in both hands. She hesitates. Then plants her lips firmly against his. A flash of white light as the essence rushes out of Rajesh and into the Asian Woman. When she lets go of him, Rajesh crumples to the floor.
The Asian Woman goes over to the Old Woman and blows her essence back into her through her ear. The Old Woman shivers as it surges into her.

Old Woman Thank God. Come, let us go and find Kumar.

The Asian Woman pauses.

What is it now?

The Asian Woman is watching Rajesh. He is shaking his head trying to get rid of the fog the experience has just left in his mind.

Rajesh Wow.

Before Rajesh can get to his feet again the Asian Woman walks over to him and takes his head in her hands again. She kisses him long and hard. Eventually she stops.

Asian Woman Strange.

Old Woman What are you doing? Do not waste your time on him – come, we must find Kumar.

Asian Woman Such an unusual sensation.

She kisses Rajesh again and again. At first Rajesh is too fazed by the whole experience to feel anything . . . and then he begins to enjoy it.

Asian Woman (*to the Old Woman*) Come, try it.

This snaps Rajesh out of his funk.

Old Woman and **Rajesh** No!

He gets to his feet and backs away from the Asian Woman who advances towards him obviously wanting more.

Rajesh No, please stop. No, please. Stop. Stop.

Old Woman Come on, we must go.

Asian Woman I didn't realise how soft and warm a person's lips were.

Rajesh Nor did I.

Asian Woman All this time I thought such things were vile and distasteful.

Rajesh So did I.

Asian Woman How wrong I was.

Rajesh How wrong I was.

Old Woman How wrong we all were.

She grabs the Asian Woman's hand and drags her towards the door.

Now come on.

Rajesh Don't go.

Old Woman We must.

Rajesh I wasn't talking to you.

Old Woman Ignore him.

Rajesh Why'd you kiss me if you're just going to leave?

Asian Woman Kiss. Such a pleasant word. I kissed you because . . . because . . .

Old Woman Because she is mad. And as we can only stay here for two days this is not worth pursuing.

Rajesh Two days? What happens in two days?

Asian Woman I have to go back.

Rajesh Back where?

Asian Woman Back to . . . back to –

She is hoping the Old Woman will help her out but the Old Woman isn't in the mood

– back to where? Where are we going in two days?

She pinches the Old Woman.

Old Woman To India. She is to marry her cousin.

Asian Woman Yes.

Rajesh Oh.

Asian Woman But I have two days.

Rajesh It's not a long time.

Asian Woman Are there any other madnesses as pleasant as a kiss?

Rajesh I think so.

Asian Woman Tell me.

Rajesh Then stay for a while.

Old Woman What is this rubbish you are talking? Come, we have more important things to do.

Rajesh Please, Auntiji, I ain't a bad bloke.

Old Woman Ha!

Rajesh You said it yourself, that I'm obedient and loyal, I wouldn't do anything wrong.

Asian Woman I trust him.

Old Woman Then do what you wish. I will find Kumar, alone if I must.

She pauses, then strolls out the door.

Asian Woman I must go with her.

Rajesh Why is she so obsessed with finding my brother?

Asian Woman They're . . . old friends.

Rajesh Old friends? (*As he speaks he begins to realise something.*) But yesterday he pretended not to know her. Then he was happy to serve her. Then he got rid of her before I came back. Oh no.

Asian Woman What?

Rajesh He's been seein' someone on the sly. He won't talk about it or tell anyone her name or anythin'. No wonder. Oh my God. Don't ever trust arty types, they're all sick in the head.

Asian Woman (*she kisses Rajesh*) I must go.

Rajesh Wait, we'll have to do something later, something, something mad, if that's what you want to do. Maybe . . . maybe –

He picks one of the fliers for Miss Moneypenny's out of the bin beside the counter

– go to Miss Moneypenny's.

Asian Woman Miss Moneypenny's?

Rajesh It's a night-club.

Asian Woman I don't know what a night-club is.

Rajesh It's a magical place, a mysterious place, a place where anything can happen and most times does.

Asian Woman It sounds enchanting.

Rajesh Meet me later at the end of the street, at about nine.

Asian Woman There is a nine at the end of the street?

Rajesh What? Nine o'clock.

Asian Woman You mean when the moon is almost at the peak of its arc?

Rajesh stares at her blankly.

Asian Woman I will be there.

Rajesh See you in a bit.

She leaves. Rajesh does a pirouette in the middle of the shop. Kumar walks back in through the door leading into the alley.

Kumar What the hell's wrong with you?

Rajesh What the hell's wrong with you you, freak?

Kumar What?

SCENE FOUR

Night, and Kumar is sitting behind the counter. He is scribbling in his sketch book when Rajesh enters the shop through the door leading into the rest of the house. He is dressed in a tight, brown, pinstriped suit that is a couple of sizes too small for him, the sleeves end above his wrists and the trousers stop above his ankles revealing his worn blue socks. He looks so painfully unfashionable that he is almost fashionable.

Kumar shakes his head as he watches his brother struggle with the suit in an attempt to make it fit.

Rajesh How do I look?

Kumar How do you look?

Rajesh Do I look okay?

Kumar You look like an idiot.

Rajesh Seriously.

Kumar Seriously?

Rajesh Yeah, what do you think?

Kumar I think you're a moral affront to my sense of what is decent. If I had a gun I'd shoot you.

Rajesh I don't believe Dad is so small. Has he started to shrink or somethin'?

Kumar That's Dad's suit?

Rajesh Yeah. I ain't got anythin' posh.

Kumar That ain't posh.

Rajesh What about you, you must have –

Kumar Forget it.

Rajesh But –

Kumar Forget it.

Rajesh Okay, this'll do. I feel good. Everythin's gonna be okay. I'm gonna be fine.

Kumar Yeah, but you look like an idiot. Where are you goin' anyway? Is that Bobby Singh havin' another one of his mind-numbin' house parties or 'sit-and-listen-to-bangra-music-for-two-hours-whilst-starin'-at-the-wall-tryin'-to-think-of-somethin'-to-say-when-none-of-you-ha ve-lives' parties?

Rajesh Miss Moneypenny's.

Kumar You're goin' to Miss Moneypenny's?

Rajesh Yeah.

Kumar With who?

Rajesh Someone.

Kumar Someone, huh?

Rajesh Yeah.

Kumar Anyone I know?

Rajesh No.

Kumar Is it some foxy lady?

Rajesh Maybe.

Kumar Which means it's one of Kulvinder's fat ugly daughters.

Rajesh No it isn't. And at least I ain't messin' about with someone who's a million years old.

Kumar I never laid a hand on that old slapper, not in any meaningful way anyway. Whatever she said she made up.

Rajesh I believe you, millions wouldn't.

Kumar Good, 'cause it's the truth.

Rajesh Anyway, don't forget to put the money in the safe, and take the bins to the end of the alley and double lock the back door.

Kumar Yeah, yeah.

Rajesh (*going over to the door*) I'll be back later.

Kumar You'll be back in about twenty minutes. No way would a class place like Miss Moneypenny's let someone as tasteless as you in.

Rajesh Whatever. And don't bother goin' through my room lookin' for any drawin's, right. I've thrown them all away.

Kumar Shithead.

> *Rajesh leaves.*
> *Kumar goes back to his sketches. For a while he draws, ostentatiously running the pencil over the page. Then he stops. He looks at what he has just done. He sighs and leans on the counter with his head in his hands.*
> *After a moment he gets up and goes into the stock room. He returns carrying a box with jars of pickled onions in it in one hand and a small step ladder in the other. He unfolds the ladder and begins to fill one of the top shelves.*
> *The door leading into the shop opens and the Old Woman comes in. Kumar almost falls off the ladder as he rushes to get down and position it between himself and the Old Woman.*

Old Woman Finally we are alone.

Kumar (*a touch of fear in his voice*) W – we're closed.

Old Woman I do not wish to buy anything.

Kumar Oh no. Hey, I don't know who you are but you ain't getting anythin' off me.

Old Woman Kumar, I want nothing from you, it is what I can give to you that matters.

Kumar You better keep your clothes on. I don't want anything off you, nothing.

Old Woman I have no desire to take my clothes off.

Kumar Thank God for small favours.

The Old Woman goes over to the counter and starts to flick through Kumar's sketch book.

What are you doin'? We're closed, go home.

Old Woman What is this pattern you keep drawing?

Kumar It's called noughts and crosses. Now will you go away.

Old Woman But where are your designs?

Kumar I keep asking myself that same thing. Auntyji, I'm gonna count to ten then I'm calling the police.

Old Woman You are too young to give up.

Kumar Well thank you for saying so. Now please, sod off.

Suddenly a shaft of bright white light appears at the back of the shop.
The Old Woman seems irresistibly drawn to it as it grows steadily larger and larger. She starts to slide across the floor towards it. She grabs onto a shelf in an attempt to stop herself being sucked in. Kumar watches all of this aghast.

Old Woman Not yet. Not yet. (*turning to Kumar*) Help me, Kumar. Help me. Please, not yet.

She is about to lose her grip on the shelf when Kumar grabs one of her hands and pulls her away from the light. The light fades and disappears.

I am discovered, surely there will be hell to pay now.

Kumar I know who you are.

Old Woman Thank God. I was afraid to tell you and now time is short we must hurry.

Kumar All those stories about little green men with big bright eyes, how wrong they were?

Old Woman Little green men?

Kumar Instead, when you turn up you're a little brown woman with beady eyes.

Old Woman I don't understand-

Kumar You don't have to play the innocent with me. I believe in you, you don't have to convince me of anythin'.

Old Woman I don't?

Kumar Not a thing. And here's me thinkin' you were some nutty old Indian woman, callin' you Auntyji and everythin'. Maybe I should be callin' you Alienji?

Old Woman Alienji?

Kumar What is this, a recon. mission? Are you scoutin' us out? Are you thinkin' about colonisin' this planet? Are you the first wave and when I wake up tomorrow will it be like 'Independence Day', fifteen mile long spaceships floatin' outside the window?

Old Woman I came –

Kumar If you're checkin' to see whether we're an intelligent life form you made such a big mistake abductin' my brother. We're not all like him, the rest of us developed beyond the stage of Neanderthal a couple of hundred thousand years ago.

Old Woman Kumar, I'm here –

Kumar Why not abduct me? Go on. Isn't that what you were going to do anyway? 'Course, the gift was meant for me, that's what you said. It *was* my focus. Thank God, you're my ticket out of shit city. I'm gonna be such a totally willin' guinea-pig, you're gonna love me. You can do whatever you want to me. Go on, take me to your spaceship.

Old Woman My spaceship?

Kumar Yeah, sure. Where is it? Parked in Alpha Centauri right? Go on take me there, take me off this planet, there's nothing for me here, I've got nothin' to lose. You can poke me and prod me and probe me as much as you want. You can even dissect me as long as you can put me back together. Come on, what do you say? Take me with you.

Old Woman I can't take you with me.

Kumar Come on, don't say that. You abducted Raj so you can abduct me, wasn't that the plan? I deserve to be abducted.

Old Woman I don't know that you are talking about.

Kumar Oh, right, not too cued up on the lingo, huh? Well when you take people off this planet and put them onto your spaceship we call that abduction. But when you do it to me we can call it somethin' like . . . a . . . sojourn. Although you don't have to bring me back. So what do you say? Take me away, please?

Old Woman Kumar, I want to help you.

Kumar Good, then you'll take me with you. Do I have to pack?

Old Woman Oh God! I'm not taking you anywhere.

Kumar You either take me with you or I'm gonna hand you over to the CIA. I know what they do to people from other planets, I've seen the Roswell tapes. Who was he anyway, a cousin of yours?

Old Woman What are you talking about aliens? What are aliens?

Kumar You're an alien. Anythin' that isn't indigenous to this planet.

Old Woman Kumar, I have only been here for five minutes and yet you have worn me out with your talking.

Kumar So you'll take me?

Old Woman No!

Kumar Then at least show me your true form.

Old Woman What?

Kumar advances towards her. The Old Woman backs away. Kumar follows her around the shop.

Kumar You don't really look like an old Indian woman, do you?

Old Woman Yes.

Kumar I bet you've got scales. Or tentacles. Or eyes on your bum. Am I right? Come, let me see. Come on. I'm open minded, you don't have to be shy around me.

Kumar chases the Old Woman in and out of the shelves. He plucks a broom from one corner and tries to push down the Old Woman's top with the handle. She pushes it aside and slaps him across the face.

Old Woman Show me some respect. I am your grand-mother.

Silence for a moment.

Kumar I hate to be a stickler for detail, but shouldn't you be in India dying?

Grandmother My body is fading but my spirit has been released.

Kumar So what does that make you, a ghost, a pseudo-ghost, a quasi-ghost, a freak?

Grandmother I'm not sure.

Kumar Great. Just my luck. Aliens could have taken me away from this shit-hole. What are you gonna do? Haunt me? Scare me? Go on, Dadiji, I dare you to. Go on, scare me.

Grandmother Kumar, I am not here to scare you. I came because we share the same dream.

Kumar Ha. I doubt that very much. How could some old biddy from India share my dream?

Grandmother But I do.

Kumar What dream is that, then? Is it the dream where I'm with Helena Christiansen and I'm playin' the velvety white cheeks of her arse like a pair of bongos? Or the dream where I'm naked and I'm walkin' down the street and everyone's havin' a party 'cause I'm that huge?

Grandmother Jinder is right. Sometimes you talk and yet not a word you say makes any sense.

Kumar Yeah, whatever, Dad doesn't always listen.

Kumar goes back to stacking the shelves.

Grandmother Kumar, I am here because all my life, ever since I was a little girl, I have designed clothes and you are the only one in our family who wants to achieve what I always dreamed of.

Kumar Am I really?

Grandmother Some years ago Jinder sent me a letter. In it he told me you where going to college, that you were studying fashion and that you wanted to be a dressmaker. The joy that I felt at that moment. I yearned to see you. I wanted to speak to you about things I had never said to anyone. I wanted to show you all the sketches that I had made and hidden away. But I knew it would not happen. I was dying. And then, when I could no longer move and I could neither hear nor see, an angel came to me. As she sat and spoke to me it seemed that we went from place to place, from city to city, from country to country without moving. I asked her how could this be and she told me the spirit is not bound as the body is. And I knew that there was only one place I wanted to see before I left this world for ever. The angel said it was wrong, that we should go straight to heaven, but I could not leave without seeing you.

Kumar (*softening towards her*) Oh.

Grandmother And now here you are before me.

Kumar Not much to look at.

Grandmother I see such a sadness in you, Kumar.

Kumar That obvious, huh?

Grandmother I tried to inspire you.

Kumar You did?

Grandmother Yes.

Kumar How?

Grandmother By giving you the fire that drove me and the images that had been in my mind for so many years.

Kumar That was the gift?

Grandmother Yes.

Kumar And you gave it to Raj by mistake.

Grandmother It is returned to me now – hopefully soon I can pass it on to you, but we must wait for my angel to return, she sneaked away without telling me where she was going, when she comes back I can pass it on to you.

Kumar I used to have that same thing inside me, Dadiji, that fire, that focus, that need to create. I didn't need anyone else's. It used to be that everywhere I looked I saw a new design. All I ever thought about was patterns and fabrics, new ways of lookin' at old things. And dreamin' that one day I would create something that would withstand the rigors of time.

Grandmother But that fire faded?

Kumar Yeah, it faded.

Grandmother But how?

Kumar Lots of reasons maybe. Or maybe because I came back here. (*Beat.*) Every day Mom or Dad or Raj will tell me I'm wasting my time. Every day. And they say it like it doesn't matter. How many rotis do you want? And oh yeah, by the way, you're wasting your time. When people come and talk to Mom and Dad they tell them that their eldest son is a doctor or a lawyer or runs his own business and I can see the sadness in their eyes 'cause they don't have anything to say. I haven't done anything, I ain't achieved anything. I'm just wasting my time. At first I used to laugh it off, I used to think what do they know, they don't know the difference between a Lacroix and a Gaultier, so sod them, forget what they say. But at some point I began to listen. Maybe my skin isn't that thick. They don't care. They think I'm a failure. But it's the only thing I can do. It's the only thing I'm good at. It would be nice if they gave a shit. But now there's only one person in the world who thinks I can do it. And Dadiji, you'd laugh if you knew how often I'm wrong.

Grandmother I believe in you.

Kumar And I love you for it, but you're a ghost.

Grandmother Don't you dare give up.

Kumar I can't keep running when I don't know where I'm running to.

Grandmother You see only what you cannot do. Look at what you can do.

Kumar But no one gives me a break.

Grandmother I stole the cloth to make my first dress. I wore it to my brother's wedding and everyone laughed at me. I ran home and cried. Then my father held my hand over a fire because he said I had brought shame on the family and he wanted to teach me my place. But I never stopped drawing. Never. You have opportunities here that I could never imagine. Here there are shops that sell everything you could want. You went to college. I could never have done that. You say your family does not believe in you. I lived in a country that never believed in me.

Kumar Thanks, Dadiji, I was feeling pretty low before you came in. Now I'm feeling suicidal.

Grandmother We are the only ones who share this passion, the only ones. One of us must succeed. And I am dying.

Kumar God, one minute no one's got any faith in me and the next I'm being crushed by the weight of expectation.

Grandmother Come here.

She grabs Kumar by one of his ears and pulls him over to the counter.

Kumar Flippin' hell, I'm still thinkin' about callin' the pigs.

Grandmother Pigs?

Kumar The police. This is physical abuse.

Once at the counter his Grandmother takes the sketch book and turns to a clean page.

Grandmother Draw.

Kumar What?

Grandmother Whatever it is you want to say.

Kumar I can't.

Grandmother You can. (*She takes the pad and pencil.*) When I was ten I saw a painting of Shah Jahan (*She draws as she speaks.*) and this is how he was dressed. Such elegance, such grace. And such power. All from the clothes he wore. Clothes that matched his eyes, his manner, his character. I wanted to capture that, I wanted to be able to create clothes that expressed a person's soul.

Kumar Yeah, those are some pretty fancy togs.

Grandmother What was it that inspired you?

Kumar I can't remember . . . something ages ago.

Grandmother (*continuing to draw*) This was my first design. It is the only one I ever made. Then I was married and I had children. I was a wife and a mother. I was never allowed to be anything else. My gift went to waste. You cannot waste yours. What was it?

Kumar I saw something on TV.

Grandmother What?

Kumar Some crap.

Grandmother Tell me.

Kumar The Royal Variety Performance. Satisfied? Mom and Dad used to force us to watch it every year. And then one year something struck me, it just sort of dawned on me. All the women were wearing the most beautiful gowns and all the men were in black suits. Black jackets, black ties, black trousers, black shoes. Dead clothes. Emotionless clothes. Like wearing cardboard boxes. And I knew I was born in the wrong era and in the wrong place. Somewhere along the way men's clothes became borin' and repressed and generally shit.

Grandmother And that is what you want to change?

Kumar Yeah, 'cause we have emotions too. I want to be able to wear stuff that looks good and feels good. I hate havin' to wear the same crap as everyone else. I want the suit to burn in hell. It's crap, everything about it is crap. I have to create something to replace it. Something fluid, something expressive, something male.

Grandmother You see, the fire is still in you. Let it out. Draw, draw, draw.

Kumar feverishly begins to draw.

SCENE FIVE

Later that same night the corner shop is dark and empty.
Suddenly the door leading out into the street bursts open and Rajesh and the Asian Woman stagger in. She is wearing a pure white sari and he is still in his Dad's suit. They are laughing and holding onto each other. The Asian Woman is holding a bottle of Hooch. She takes

a swig from it and then bursts into laughter for no apparent reason. Rajesh puts a finger to his lips and shushes the Asian Woman. They both try to hold in their laughter as Rajesh turns on one of the lights.

As soon as he can see what he is doing Rajesh goes behind the counter and brings out the small portable radio. He puts in a tape and presses play. Harsh bangra music explodes from the small machine. The Asian Woman bursts into laughter. Rajesh quickly reduces the volume and then comes out from behind the counter wiggling his hips and waving his arms. The Asian Woman watches him perform his slinky moves for a moment then she chips in with some of her own wild gyrations. They weave around each other like Fred Astaire and Ginger Rogers on speed, their contortions more alarming than graceful.

When the track stops they fall against the counter, exhausted. They laugh at each other and themselves. They are both crap dancers and they know it, but it doesn't seem to matter.

A slower, more romantic piece of music begins to play.

They look at each other. Suddenly there is a shy hesitancy in their laughter. They have become very self-conscious. Rajesh takes the Asian Woman by the hand and tries to lead her in a slow dance but as neither of them knows what they are doing he ends up stepping on her toes. She hops around holding her foot. Rajesh looks mortified. The Asian Woman loses her balance. She almost falls but Rajesh catches her. He holds her in his arms.

A moment.

The Asian Woman pushes herself away from Rajesh suddenly, as though she has just come to some shocking self-realisation. She walks over to one side of the shop. Rajesh moves to the other, his head bowed, his shoulders hunched, a dejected air about him.

In the background the music continues to play in synch with Rajesh and the Asian Woman's actions.

The Asian Woman keeps glancing over to Rajesh; it is obvious she is fighting some inner battle. Rajesh stands with his back to her. Eventually, hesitantly, the Asian Woman makes her way over to him. She gently touches his back. He turns. They look at each other for a moment.

Finally they kiss.

Rajesh What's your name?

Asian Woman My name?

Rajesh I don't know your name.

Asian Woman Angel.

Rajesh kisses her once more.

Act Two

SCENE ONE

The next morning. Kumar is standing behind the counter with his Grandmother. He is still wearing the same clothes he was wearing last night. There is a mug of coffee next to him. They are both bent over their own sketch pads as they scribble away in unison.

Grandmother (*glancing over to Kumar's pad*) Isn't that a little short? Perhaps if you make it longer here and here.

Kumar Dadiji, be free and be wild. It would look great with that cropped top of yours.

He flicks through her pad until he comes to the design he wants and then he pushes the two pads together so his Grandmother can fully appreciate how well the two items go together.

Kumar See?

His Grandmother just throws her arms around him as she accepts the truth.

I don't believe we've done it. Two whole new lines of clothes all in one night. You're a little wonder, Dadiji, you really are.

Grandmother I have not felt this excited since my mother managed to talk old Choree into giving me a job in his clothes shop when I was fourteen. He was a fine tailor but not very adventurous and of course he was not too pleased when I stole some of his cloth.

Kumar His loss.

65

Grandmother He had a book in his office that detailed every fashion from all over the world. Many hours I spent looking through its pages and marvelling at the dresses and suits of countries I could not even imagine. I would dream that some day the shop would belong to me and then I would change the way people dressed.

Kumar To create something that would withstand the rigors of time. This Choree sounds like a rogue. They're all rogues. You work for someone else, Dadiji, and you have to compromise, that's the nature of things, that's the way things are. I don't fancy going back to all those people who told me to get lost.

Grandmother Do not let your pride hinder you, you will need other people's help.

Kumar Other people's help, yes, but not their interference. So many people told me what I couldn't do, I began to believe them. And it's not as if I'm shithead Pierre. Pierre with his penthouse flat. Pierre with his rich Mum and Dad. Pierre with his café culture mates. Pierre who can do whatever he pleases 'cause he sucks up to the right people. Damn you to hell, Pierre, you're crap!

Grandmother Who is this Pierre you shout at?

Kumar Some shithead.

He begins to pace about the shop.

Kumar Those designs are too good to hand over to some fanny-faced scavenger who's just gonna ruin them.

Grandmother But surely there is a way things should be done. Maybe when you have a little more money you can be so brave.

Kumar Don't believe that for a minute, Dadiji, that's the way everyone wants you to think so they can batter you down into thinking like they think, believin' what they believe. If you want to change the way people dress you've gotta be radical from the off.

Grandmother But what can you do?

Kumar Make do with what we have. That's what Dad's always saying. Did you teach him that?

Grandmother I think that he learnt from his father. We were not very well off when the children were young.

Kumar I always thought it was just an easy way of saying no when we wanted more toys. But maybe . . .

Kumar stops his pacing. He looks around at the shop. He smiles.

Kumar You know what I see?

Grandmother No, tell me.

Kumar goes over to one wall.

Kumar I see a huge floral display up here. Nothin' too elaborate. Just somethin' that would set the whole thing off, give the place a touch of atmosphere.

Grandmother A touch of atmosphere?

Kumar goes over to the door leading into the street.

Kumar And maybe . . . maybe a huge archway over here, make the place look bigger, imposin', give the proceedin's weight to them, an official stamp if you will.

Grandmother I am beginning to see.

Kumar And paintings, lots of Indian paintings.

Grandmother Do you also see candles?

Kumar Dadiji, it's like you read my mind. Yes, candles. Lots of candles. Candles everywhere. I've had a thing for candles for a long time. And the catwalk can flow down here, gently curvin', meanderin' like a river.

Grandmother And incense sticks, there must be incense sticks. And the walls must be repainted, this colour won't do. And music, there must be music, I could never see my shop without also hearing the music that would be playing in it.

Kumar Damn right. God, it's all so obvious I should have thought about it a long time ago. This will give us the freedom to do whatever we please and not be slaves to talentless money men. It's like makin' the impossible possible. Like grabbin' hold of life and doin' somethin' that's gonna count, somethin' that's gonna make a statement. We're gonna do somethin' that's gonna let the world know we're here. Dadiji, we're gonna turn the corner shop into a haute couture house!

He picks up his Grandmother and spins her around.

Grandmother But Kumar?

Kumar Yeah?

Grandmother What is a haute couture house?

Kumar Like Choree's shop except better.

Grandmother Perfect, everything is becoming as I dreamed it would be.

Kumar It shouldn't be too hard, a little paint, a bit of reorganising, get rid of these shelves of course, and we're sorted.

Grandmother Kumar.

Kumar (*muttering to himself*) Would a marble effect be too much? A more subtle colour. Ambient, that's the key.

Grandmother Kumar.

Kumar Do you think I'd be pushin' the boat out a bit too far if I tried to build an extension?

Grandmother I must leave you for a little while.

Kumar Why?

Grandmother I must find my angel, she will be thinking that I have deserted her and she will be losing her mind with worry.

Kumar Do you have to?

Grandmother Yes, I promised her I would not come here. I must find her and tell her that we have been discovered, she will know what to do.

Kumar Well, don't be gone too long.

Grandmother I won't.

She leaves. As the door swings shut Rajesh enters the shop through the door leading into the rest of the house. He is in a very chirpy mood.

Rajesh Top of the mornin' to you bro, how's it hangin'?

Kumar Raj, we're turnin' the shop into a haute couture house.

Rajesh No, we're not.

He starts to skip around Kumar, playfully throwing punches at him but never making contact. Kumar tries to ignore him and ploughs on regardless.

Kumar It's the best thing for us to do, especially as the shop's gonna close.

Rajesh No, it isn't.

Kumar Yes, it is. If we turn it into a couture house you can worry about the books, the money, the hiring and sellin' and I'll worry about designin' the clothes and gettin' them made.

Rajesh laughs.

Kumar What's so funny, minge-mouth?

Rajesh Oh, I was just thinkin'.

Kumar Thinkin' about what?

Rajesh Thinkin' about all the other crazy schemes you've had.

Kumar There haven't been any other crazy schemes.

Rajesh Like the time you created that range of see-through rubber beachwear for the old Indian woman at the community centre.

Kumar I was tryin' to encourage them to be proud of what they are.

Rajesh Or the time you tried to convince Dad to invest in that design of yours, that one you thought was gonna be the next big thing, those low-cut trousers.

Kumar If women can flash their cleavage about I thought it was high time men could show off some of their assets.

Rajesh No one wants a face full of pubes and I don't believe you modelled one in front of Mum and Dad. Mum had nightmares for a month.

Kumar Anyway, my days of wanderin' through the wilderness of creative limbo are over.

Rajesh mimes punching Kumar repeatedly in the stomach before topping the attack off by pretending to knee him in the nuts.
Kumar finally cracks.

Will you piss off, you idiot, I'm being serious!

Rajesh You can be as serious as you want, you can't do anythin' to the shop.

Kumar Why?

Rajesh What do you mean why? 'Cause it ain't yours.

Kumar I always thought it was ours?

Rajesh If there's one person who has least say in what happens to the shop it's you.

Kumar But it's so obviously the right thing to do.

Rajesh The shop belongs to Dad. We can't do anythin' to it unless he says so.

Kumar You want me to phone Dad up in India and ask him if we can turn the shop into a couture house?

Rajesh It's the only way.

Kumar He'll say no.

Rajesh 'Course he'll say no, it's a stupid idea. We've got bills to pay, a mortgage to pay. We've got months of unsold stock in the back and months of stock on order. We've got year-long contracts with one baker and two farmers so we can sell organic food. Dad's just spent a couple of grand so we can start hiring out videos next month and he's talking to Camelot about getting' a lottery machine.

Kumar Talk about a negative attitude.

Rajesh So forget it.

Kumar But –

Rajesh Forget it.

Kumar But –

Rajesh Shut up.

Kumar But last night Dadiji's spirit came and inspired me and we've decided that turning the shop into a couture house is the only way forward. It's destined to happen.

Rajesh Are you nuts?

Kumar That old woman who's been, it's Dadiji. She came here with an angel. She came here to inspire me. You weren't abducted, you arse.

Rajesh You can make up as much crap as you want to, right, but it isn't gonna convince me to turn the shop into anythin'.

Kumar It's the truth.

Rajesh 'Course it is. What are you tryin' to hide? Did you snog her?

Kumar What? Why would I snog my own grandmother you sick git? Don't move. She just left to find the other angel. I'll go get her and she'll tell you.

Kumar rushes out of the door. As it closes behind him Angel stumbles into the shop through the door leading into the rest of the house. She is in a bad way, obviously suffering from the excesses of last night. She is dressed in one of Rajesh's old pyjamas.

Angel Oh my head, my poor, poor head. What is happening to me? Oh, it feels as if I am dying, if that were possible. (*She retches.*) Oh Lord be merciful.

Rajesh Don't puke up. Take deep breaths, deep breaths.

Rajesh picks up the bin from beside the counter and starts to follow Angel around with it.

Angel I want to crawl into a corner and fade away.

Rajesh I told you not to drink so much Hooch.

Angel It feels as though Lucifer himself has stuck his tongue down my throat. Oh Lord, take pity on me, do not punish me so.

Rajesh I don't think God's got anything to do with it. You've got a hangover.

Angel A hangover? This is normal? I'm not being punished?

Rajesh No, you just drank too much.

Angel God be praised.

Rajesh Some people say the way to get rid of a hangover is to drink more alcohol.

Angel More? Surely that would be tempting fate. Do you have any more of that sweet nectar? That Hooch?

Rajesh Sure, we sell it, there's crates of it in the back.

Angel Then bring me a whole crate.

She retches once more. Rajesh shoves the bin into her face.

Get that smelly thing out of my face.

Rajesh Let's forget about the Hooch. Do you want a coffee or something?

Angel Will a coffee cure the pain?

Rajesh I have no idea, I've never had a hangover.

Angel Get me one then. But also bring me a Hooch just to be safe.

Rajesh disappears into the back of the house.
Angel goes to get herself a chair and notices a couple of bottles of Hooch on one of the shelves. She makes sure she is alone and then she takes one of the bottles. She knocks the top off against the shelf and then downs the entire bottle in one go. She is half way through her second bottle when Rajesh returns with a mug of coffee and a paracetamol.

Rajesh What are you doin'?

He puts the coffee and tablet on the counter and wrestles Angel away from the Hooch. She tries to resist but Rajesh eventually gets the bottle off her.

Angel Don't be such a greebo.

Rajesh What's a greebo?

Angel I don't know, someone in Miss Moneypenny's said it.

Rajesh lowers Angel into a chair and then hands her the coffee and paracetamol.

(*looking at the paracetamol*) What is this?

Rajesh A paracetamol.

Angel What do I do with it?

Rajesh What do you mean? You swallow it.

Angel throws the pill into her mouth and takes a big draught of coffee.

Angel Oh, that tastes vile.

Rajesh Sorry, we only had Nescafé.

Angel I don't feel any better. I need more Hooch. Go get me more alcohol.

Rajesh It takes a while, I think.

Angel cradles the mug in her hands as she waits for the pain to abate.

Rajesh My brother said a weird thing just now.

Angel Did he?

Rajesh He said that old woman you came in with yesterday was the spirit of our dying grandmother.

Angel Why would he think that?

Rajesh Apparently she came here last night and inspired him. Now they want to change the shop into some kind of fashion house.

Angel Oh.

Rajesh You know you said they were friends, right? Well they're just friend friends aren't they and not friieeends. Know what I mean?

Angel No.

Rajesh Well, who is she?

Angel A stubborn, pig-headed busy-body.

Rajesh Do you know her family?

Angel I'm beginning to know them.

Rajesh Maybe I should call Parminder at the temple, he could look after her until we find out who she is. Or maybe I could beat the truth out of Ku. Then again, maybe the truth is just too scary.

Angel She's harmless.

Rajesh Anyway, forget about them. What are we gonna do about us?

Angel Us?

Rajesh How are we gonna stop you havin' to go to India to marry your cousin?

Angel My cousin? Oh.

Rajesh Do you want me to talk to your parents? I think they'd like me, most girls' parents like me. I'll take your Dad to the pub, give him a game of darts or cards or whatever he plays, soften him up, right, and then tell him about us and tell him there's no way you can marry your cousin, not now. But we better act soon, when do you go, tomorrow? Whatever you do don't get on a plane with them, right? I've heard loads of stories where parents steal their kids' passports and won't let them out of India until they marry who they want. What does he look like anyway, your cousin? Is he a bit ugly?

Angel He's . . . I . . . Raj, I have to tell you something.

Rajesh What?

Angel I'm . . . you don't have any mental illnesses do you?

Rajesh No.

Angel And everyone in your family is sane?

Rajesh I think so, although Ku's a bit of a dick.

Angel Can I ask you something?

Rajesh 'Course.

Angel Do you really believe in God? Or saints? Do you think prophets had anything worthwhile to say? And if I told you the big bang was a cosmic sneeze would you think me a fool?

Rajesh What's that got to do with anythin'? What are you talkin' about?

Angel Raj, I'm . . . I'm an angel.

A beat.

Your brother was telling the truth. The old woman is your grandmother.

Rajesh Don't say that.

Angel Sorry.

Rajesh Oh bollocks.

Angel We shouldn't have lied to you.

Rajesh Then why did you?

Angel I thought your brain might implode if you found out the truth.

Rajesh Why would my brain implode?

Angel People can't always cope with things like this.

Rajesh So you thought kissin' me, goin' to Miss Moneypenny's with me and spendin' the night with me would make it easier to cope with?

Angel It wasn't a kiss.

Rajesh It felt like a kiss to me.

Angel Don't shout, my head hurts.

Rajesh So you're really an angel?

Angel Yes.

Rajesh What kind of angel does what we did on my television last night?

Angel A foolish one.

Rajesh Well, if you don't tell anyone I won't.

Angel I cannot stay.

Rajesh Why?

Angel As soon as your grandmother draws her last breath, we will have to leave. We won't have a choice.

Rajesh When's that gonna be?

Angel Soon.

Rajesh starts to tidy up around the shop.

Rajesh What was the point?

Angel Of what?

Rajesh Of spendin' one night together?

Angel It was something new for us both. I've existed since the dawn of time and going to Miss Moneypenny's was the most fun I've had. It was a laugh.

Rajesh A laugh? I've just found out that my first sexual experience was with someone who isn't even human and you've got a massive hangover. Who's laughin'?

Angel Why are you acting this way?

Rajesh What way?

Angel As though it is all my fault.

Rajesh 'Cause it is.

Angel How?

Rajesh You kissed me.

Angel It wasn't a kiss. Oh, my head. And I saw the way you looked at me when I walked in.

Rajesh What way was that then?

Angel Lasciviously.

Rajesh looks at her blankly.

It means –

Rajesh I know what it means, and I'm sure I wasn't doin' it.

Angel Your tongue almost fell out.

Rajesh You probably used some angel magic to entrap me.

Angel Oh please.

Rajesh I've read stories about it, right, angels encin' sailors to their death.

Angel That's mermaids you fool.

Rajesh Angels, mermaids, what's the difference?

Angel Mermaids have fins.

Rajesh Whatever, it was a waste of bloody time.

Angel You think what you want. When I get back I'm probably going to get an earful from the Angel of Peace and God's going to be in a mood, but I don't care. I enjoyed myself, I had fun last night for the first time.

Rajesh Good for you.

Angel I owe it to you.

Rajesh I'm bloody honoured.

Angel Thank you.

Rajesh My pleasure.

A pause.

I just want you to stay.

Angel I can't.

Rajesh So you get to go to heaven and I have to stay here alone.

Angel I have to go to heaven alone and you get to stay here. This isn't such a bad place is it. If I could, I'd stay.

Rajesh But you can't or won't, so just go.

A beat. Angel gets up to leave but stumbles over some boxes.

Angel This worthless shop.

Rajesh The shop isn't worthless.

Angel It's falling apart.

Rajesh No it isn't.

Angel (*getting up*) It's not important.

Rajesh It is important. The shop's the only thing that's important.

Angel The shop and everything else.

Rajesh No, just the shop. Here's where everythin' makes sense. You know in the last five years the only change we've made, right, is addin' an organic food section. Between these four walls the world doesn't matter.

Angel But it should.

Rajesh Why, so you can learn to live with disappointment? I remember when I was a kid and Dad taught me how to do the books and Mum taught me how to deal with the stock and the customers. That was years ago and nothin's changed, right, it's still exactly the same. And the people who come in here, sometimes they do it like clockwork. They come in at practically the same time every day or every other day and buy the same thing. Mr Pierce from over the road, he comes in here every mornin' while I'm still stockin' the shelves and he always buys a packet of crisps and a Flake, right. The Flake is for this woman at work who he fancies but has never told. He knows she likes Flakes, that's why he always buys one. But he never gives it to her. He always ends up eatin' it himself, and then he'll come in the next mornin' and buy another one and say maybe today. Four years he's been doin' that. And there's Mrs Gupta who comes in just before seven when we reduce the price of the bread, right, and she always gets herself a loaf of white, thin sliced. She used to pick me and Ku up from primary school when we were kids and Mum and Dad were too busy. Now she can hardly walk, she has to use a zimmer-frame. But she hobbles in, talks for a while, then hobbles out. It takes her half an hour to get here and half an hour to get back, but she won't let us help her and she doesn't want us to deliver the bread. And Mrs Jones from number thirteen, right, she always comes in here at about quarter to six dependin' on the buses and she always buys her fags and a bottle of milk. I can't even remember when she first came in, it's been so long ago. But now I know her and she knows me. Like I know that for ages her and Mr Jones were tryin' to have a kid, right, but somehow it just never happened. Then they were gonna try some artificial way but when they went to the doctor to have a check up he found somethin' out. She has cancer. She still comes in for her fags: I let her have them for free. (*He is tidying up the shelf with the cheap toilet paper on it.*) I know all these people, right, and they know me, I've grown up with them.

Angel And you want to grow old with them?

Rajesh Workin' in this shop's the only thing I've ever done, it's the only thing I know, it's the only thing I'm good at.

Suddenly the shelf collapses and rolls of cheap toilet paper fall about his feet.

Shit.

He bends down, obviously meaning to gather the toilet paper up. But he stops. Silence for a moment.

Stay.

Angel I can't.

Rajesh The . . . the stupid shop's gonna close. Dad said when he comes back from India we're gonna have to have a talk. I already know what he's gonna say, we've been losing money for months. If you leave and the shop closes I ain't gonna have anythin'. I don't know what I'm gonna do. What am I gonna do?

Rajesh stands in the middle of the shop looking lost and exhausted. Angel goes to him and holds him as tightly as she can.

Angel I met a wise man once, he was a philosopher from Greece, I think. He was chasing a young boy when he stopped and we began to talk. He said it is always better to be at the beginning of a great adventure than at the end.

Rajesh Sounds like somethin' Ku would say.

Angel What was it he wanted to do?

Rajesh I don't know what he was talkin' about.

Angel At least you won't have to put up with God's wrath for the next millennia.

Rajesh Bad, huh?

Angel She can have such a face on Her when She's in a mood.

Rajesh Heaven doesn't sound all white and fluffy.

Angel You don't know the half of it. Some day you'll find out, for now concentrate on today.

Suddenly the door leading out into the street bursts open and Rajesh's Grandmother strides in. Kumar follows quickly behind her.

Grandmother Rajesh, what is this Kumar has been telling me? I will not allow you to destroy his passion as mine was. Perhaps there is a place for your narrow-mindedness, but it is not here. I might be old but I can still take my slipper to you if that is what it takes.

Kumar Here Dadiji, use one of mine.

He takes off one of his huge silver boots and slaps it into his Grandmother's hand. She advances towards Rajesh menacingly.

Rajesh Dadiji, calm down. Let's do it.

Kumar What?

Rajesh Let's turn the corner shop into a haute c-c-c-whatever house.

Kumar But you said we shouldn't.

Rajesh Now I think we should.

Kumar Great, brill, wonderful, let's do it.

Rajesh We're gonna need a lot of money.

Kumar Don't worry about that, I have the perfect plan to get lots of money quickly. A plan that has absolutely no chance of failure.

Rajesh What?

SCENE TWO

An elaborate dance sequence in which Kumar, Rajesh, their Grandmother and Angel dismantle the corner shop all to some beautifully cheesy, easy-listening music.

They throw cans to each other, juggle pickles between them and pass around the cheap toilet paper and lay it to rest in a cardboard box. They dance with each and a broom. At one point the two women hide and the brothers pretend to look for them, a sequence right out of a million Bollywood films. When the brothers find Angel and Grandmother everyone is suitably surprised.

By the time they have finished dancing the corner shop is very bare. The counter is moved to the middle of the room and there are boxes stacked against one wall.

Saturday night, and Rajesh is stacking the last of the cans in a box.

The portable radio is on the counter and the National Lottery live draw is on.

Radio Announcer . . . and that was St Augustine's brass band . . .

Kumar comes rushing in through the door leading to the rest of the house.

Kumar Where are they?

Rajesh They'll be here.

Kumar They should have been here half an hour ago.

Rajesh You're the one who sent them, so stop worryin'.

Kumar I drew them a map, didn't I?

Rajesh You should have gone with them, they've probably gotten lost.

Kumar Don't say that. Anyway, I had to put the finishin' touches to those bucket boots. They're gonna be a show-stopper. I can already visualise most of parliament wearin' them.

Rajesh Great.

Kumar Come on, where are they? God, I'm so stressed I think I'm becomin' sterile. I can feel my seed dyin'. Where are they? (*Pause.*) You haven't told me about you and Angel.

Rajesh Not much to tell.

Kumar You're my younger brother, I just want to make sure everythin' went okay.

Rajesh Miss Moneypenny's was nice.

Kumar Goood.

Rajesh We had some fish and chips from that Greek place, the one with –

Kumar Okay, maybe I'm bein' too subtle. Take me to after Miss Moneypenny's and after fish and chips and pick it up right about when you started to take her clothes off.

Rajesh I ain't tellin' you about that.

Kumar Oh come on, please. You're the only person I'm ever gonna know who's slept with an angel. I need to know more. Come on, tell me, please.

Rajesh No.

Kumar Was she demandin'? Was she easily pleased? I need to know.

Rajesh She was somethin' special.

Kumar That's it?

Rajesh That's it.

Kumar Well that's hardly gonna fill a chapter in my memoirs.

Rajesh Don't you go writin' about it either.

Kumar Don't worry, anonymity is guaranteed. Anyway, I was gonna replace your name with mine.

Radio Announcer Bruce, could you please start the machine . . .

Kumar and Rajesh rush over to the radio.

Kumar They're about to draw the balls. Where are they?

The door leading into the shop bursts open and Angel and Grandmother rush in. Angel is brandishing a lottery ticket.

Angel I got it!

Kumar About time.

Grandmother The delay was my fault. I tripped over the pavement outside some fool's house.

Kumar Okay, okay. Give that here.

He snatches the ticket off Angel and looks at the numbers.
Rajesh looks over his shoulder.

Rajesh (*dubiously*) Those are the winnin' numbers?

Kumar Well, they've got as much chance of bein' picked as any others.

Rajesh They have no chance of bein' picked.

Kumar Come on, who's more in tune with all the cosmic forces than an angel and . . . miscellaneous? Sorry, Dadiji, you're neither one nor the other yet. We can't lose, we've got God on our side.

Angel I don't know about that.

Kumar throws his arms around his Grandmother and Angel. There is a big smile on his face, he is sure they are all on the verge of becoming millionaires.

Kumar Come on everybody, let's have a little bit of faith.

Radio Announcer This week's first number is forty-five, making its seventh appearance and last picked in October. The second number is thirty-six, last picked four weeks ago and making its eighth appearance. The third number is ten, making its nineteenth appearance and unlucky for some. (*Aside:* Ten isn't unlucky? I thought it was.) The fourth number is thirty-eight making only its second appearance and last seen in May. The fifth number is twenty-seven, last seen in January and the number of blackbirds baked in a pie. (*Aside:* It's four and twenty blackbirds?) The sixth number is thirty last seen in March and making its fifteenth appearance in the National Lottery. And this week's bonus ball is seven. So those numbers again-

Rajesh turns the radio off.

Kumar I don't believe it. What the hell just happened? We didn't get a single number.

Rajesh You don't believe it? Angel and Dadiji pick one, two, three, four, five and six and you don't believe it?

Kumar Have you ever done the lottery before?

Angel Of course not. I tried to fill in the whole form but the woman at the shop wouldn't let me.

Kumar You don't think you could have shared that choice bit of information with me earlier?

Angel Isn't it obvious?

Rajesh And that was your master plan?

Kumar Oh my God, my life's a livin' hell. We might as well pack up and go home.

Rajesh We have to brainstorm. Either we come up with some ideas on how to get some money, right, or this is never gonna work.

He gets some paper and a pen from under the counter.

Okay, give me some ideas.

Silence.

Okay, I'll start. Let's try the Arts Council, the local Arts Board and the Lottery Fundin'.

Kumar They're all a bunch of clueless knobs. They only fund stuff if it's crap and/or worthy.

Rajesh Let me fill out the forms this time

Kumar Okay, but let's see if we can milk the fact that we're Asian and live in the inner city. It might be worth pretendin' that you're gay, disabled and have a hump; the more of a minority you are the more they'll love you.

Rajesh All right then. How about this, we could sell all the stock off at a discount price. Have a kind of car boot sale, right, but sell canned food and Tampons.

Kumar Great, we can do that tomorrow. Come on, ladies, don't hold back.

Grandmother Isn't there anyone we could ask to help us?

Kumar Not around here, word would get back to Mum and Dad and that would kill the party.

Angel I'm sorry, I'm not very aware of human affairs. Aren't there any . . . rich landowners you could ask?

Kumar A rich landowner. Do we know any rich landowner?

Rajesh shrugs.

Rajesh Okay, that's more of a Plan B. But I tell you what we could do.

Kumar What?

Rajesh We could trip over the pavement outside Mr Mittar's house, right, and sue the council, people are doin' that all the time.

Kumar Brill, love it.

Grandmother Couldn't you boys work in the fields?

Kumar Dadiji, that's a great plan with only one small drawback; there aren't any fields in the middle of this city and what fields there are ain't the kind of places you can get a job. Unless it was a job collectin' dog turds and I don't think they give you any money at the recyclin' place for handin' that in. So put that in the Plan B list.

Rajesh Let's get everyone we know to do a sponsored somethin'.

> *While the brothers are coming up with crazy schemes to make money their Grandmother watches them with a smile on her face.*

Kumar A sponsored . . . snog. Who can snog who for the longest. Who can snog a pressure plate the hardest and who can create the most liquid durin' a fifteen minute snog. Brilliant idea. I've got loads of mates who have been waitin' for just that kind of chance.

> *Their Grandmother takes Angel by the arm. She leads Angel away from the boys.*

Rajesh I was thinkin' more of a run or walk, but as long as we make some money. How about this, right? Daljit and Billy are gettin' married soon.

Kumar Yeah?

Rajesh How much money is there floatin' around at an Indian weddin'?

Grandmother (*to Angel*) I think it is time for us to leave.

Kumar Loads. I see what you're sayin'. You want us to rob them.

Angel (*looking at Rajesh*) Must we? Can't we stay just a while longer?

Grandmother They do not need us now.

Rajesh No, I don't want to rob them. We get them to invest that money in the shop.

Kumar But won't they have to give it to their parents?

Rajesh Daljit and Billy wouldn't do that, they'd want to keep it.

Kumar It's worth a try. But put robbin' them down as a Plan B, just to be safe.

The lights in the shop fade.
  A bright white light appears at the back of the shop and grows steadily larger and larger.

Angel It seems that we have no choice.

Rajesh What's goin' on?

Angel It's time for us to go.

Kumar and **Rajesh** What?

A knock at the door causes them all to freeze.

Angel Oh no, it is the Angel of Peace, he has finally come to execute some terrible judgement.

Kumar goes over to a window and pulls back the curtain draped across it so he can see outside.

Kumar Shit, it's worse than that. It's Mr Mittar.

Rajesh I bet he's come to find out why the shop's closed.

Kumar Shithead.

Grandmother We must hurry.

Mr Mittar continues to knock at the door for a while, then seems to give up.
  Grandmother and Angel walk over to the light. The boys follow them.

Kumar I don't want you to go.

Grandmother I have helped you as much as I can.

Kumar Dad always talked about goin' to India. I just wasn't too fussed, for some reason I never thought I'd find someone like you there.

Grandmother We were together for a moment, a moment I waited eighty years for. Come.

They hold each other. Once Kumar has let go of her, she turns to Rajesh.

Forgive me, Rajesh, I judged you harshly.

Rajesh That's okay.

Grandmother Watch over him.

Rajesh I will.

Grandmother (*throwing her arms around them both*) You are such fine boys. Jinder grew up to be a good father.

Rajesh (*to Angel*) See you in heaven?

Angel I hope so.

Rajesh There's a million things I want to say to you. Goodbye isn't one of them.

Angel I wish I was human.

Rajesh So do I.

He kisses her on the cheek.

Angel I don't want to go.

Rajesh wipes a tear from her eye.

Tears for the first time.

They look at each other. A beat. Angel takes Grandmother's hand and the two of them turn and face the light.

Grandmother My hands are shaking like a little girl's. Look in my pad, I have left you something.

She and Angel step into the light and disappear. The light fades and quickly vanishes.

Silence for a moment as the lights in the shop come back up.

Kumar goes over to the counter where his Grandmother's sketch pad is lying next to the radio. He opens it.

Kumar Look at this.

He shows Rajesh what their Grandmother has drawn. It is a logo that consists of 'Sindhu & Sindhu', written so the brothers' surnames form the wings of an angel, and the '&' forms the body.

Oh crap. Why did they have to go?

Rajesh Nothin' lasts forever.

Kumar We're doin' the right thing, aren't we?

Rajesh How'd you mean?

Kumar By turnin' the shop into a fashion house? We're not makin' one of my stupid mistakes are we?

Rajesh I don't think so.

Kumar I mean it's such a crazy thing to do. Maybe we should . . .

Rajesh What?

Kumar Nothin'. We could always change it back? If it doesn't work, we'd still have enough time to change it back before Mum and Dad got back, wouldn't we?

Rajesh I think we're doin' the right thing.

Kumar Good. Keep tellin' me that.

Rajesh You know somethin'?

Kumar What?

Rajesh For so long I've always thought that every word you said was bollocks. All your talk about clothes, and fashion, and models, all that, right, I thought was complete bollocks. And that stuff you say about wantin' to create somethin' that will withstand the rigors of time, that I thought was bollocks on a biblical scale. But now . . . now it doesn't seem like bollocks any more.

Kumar It ain't bollocks to have a dream.

Rajesh I guess not.

Mr Mittar starts to knock on the door again.

Kumar That shithead isn't gonna go away.

Rajesh One of us is gonna have to go and talk to him.

Kumar You do it.

Rajesh What am I gonna tell him?

Kumar Tell him . . . we're closed 'cause we got robbed. Or tell him we're just tryin' a new look and we're in the middle of refurbishin'. No, better still, tell him some aliens came and stole our stock and left the place covered in green slime.

The two brothers smile.
In one of the back rooms the telephone begins to ring.

Rajesh I'll tell him we just heard Dadiji had died, that's why we closed early.

Kumar Yeah, that's probably the best.

Rajesh goes over to the door.

Rajesh As soon as he's gone let's start phonin' people and writin' some letters.

Kumar Mum and Dad are gonna shit in their pants when they get back.

Rajesh opens the door a crack and slips outside.
Kumar goes to answer the phone.